What's It Like?

Life and Culture in Britain Today

JOANNE COLLIE
& ALEX MARTIN

CAMBRIDGE UNIVERSITY PRESS
Cambridge, New York, Melbourne, Madrid, Cape Town, Singapore, São Paulo

Cambridge University Press
The Edinburgh Building, Cambridge CB2 2RU, UK

www.cambridge.org
Information on this title: www.cambridge.org/9780521586627

First published 2000
5th printing 2006

Printed in Dubai by Oriental Press

A catalogue record for this publication is available from the British Library

ISBN-13 978-0-521-58662-7 Student's Book
ISBN-10 0-521-58662-3 Student's Book

ISBN-13 978-0-521-58661-0 Teacher's Book
ISBN-10 0-521-58661-5 Teacher's Book

ISBN-13 978-0-521-58660-3 Cassette
ISBN-10 0-521-58660-7 Cassette

CONTENTS

Shetland Islands

Orkney Islands

Outer Hebrides

Inverness

Aberdeen

SCOTLAND

Dundee

Glasgow

Edinburgh

NORTHERN IRELAND

Belfast

Newcasle upon Tyne

Lake District

Durham

Yorkshire

Scarborough

Isle of Man

Blackpool

Leeds

York

Dublin

Liverpool

Manchester

Caernarvon

Chester

Sheffield

ENGLAND

Nottingham

Norwich

WALES

Birmingham

Leicester

East Anglia

Coventry

Cambridge

Swansea

Bedford

Cardiff

Oxford

Bristol

Windsor

London

Bath

Southampton

Canterbury

Exeter

Cornwall

Plymouth

Brighton

Hastings

Isle of Wight

100527851

UNIT 1

WHAT IS BRITAIN?

A | BRITAIN AND THE BRITISH

1 When you think about Britain, what things come into your mind? Write down as many things as you can. With a partner or the class, compare your lists.
Place the items in one of the four categories.

England   Scotland   Wales   Northern Ireland

Do your lists indicate that you know more about one country rather than another?

2 Look again at your lists. How many items do you think are typical of the life of ordinary people who live in Britain today? How many are traditional items or stereotypes?

Take it in turns to describe the photos on the opposite page. Which ones represent stereotypes, and which represent ordinary life today?

What about your country? Are there traditional items that people associate with it, or stereotypes? How close are they to the ordinary life of most people?

3 How much do you know about Britain and the British? Can you choose the right endings to the following statements?

1 The parliament of Scotland was joined with that of England and Wales by the Act of Union in 1707, but the parliament of Ireland remained separate until
  a 1750   **b** 1800   **c** 1900

2 After that, the whole of Ireland was considered part of Britain until 1920 when the British government separated the island into two parts and
  a Northern Ireland remained as part of Britain   **b** Southern Ireland remained as part of Britain
  c Both parts became independent countries

3 In 1997, the people of Scotland voted to have their own parliament, while the Welsh, by a much smaller majority, decided to
  a have their own parliament too   **b** separate from the United Kingdom   **c** keep sending their representatives to the parliament in London

4 The British flag, the Union Jack, combines the flags of
  a all four countries   **b** England and Scotland   **c** England, Scotland and Ireland

St George's Cross

The Dragon of Cadwallader

St Andrew's Cross

St Patrick's Cross

5 The Welsh national symbol is the leek or
the daffodil, but the symbol for Scotland is
a the rose **b** the thistle **c** the shamrock

Check your answers with the teacher.

Leek

Daffodil

Rose

Thistle

Shamrock

4 Britain is a country in transition, with relationships between its four nations evolving rapidly.
What about your country? Is it evolving or relatively stable?

5 Read these three questions, then find answers in the article below.

a Who finds the label 'British' least acceptable: the English, the Scots or the Welsh?
b What four things have contributed to creating a sense of British identity?
c Why do some people feel that 'Britishness' is no longer a useful concept?

British Unity in Diversity

What is Britishness? Is it more than the sum of its parts – or less? Many Scots and not a few Welsh believe that Britishness is no more than a disguised version of Englishness. I have just visited three towns with the same name – one each in Scotland, Wales and England – to try to discover whether there is an overarching sense of identity that it still makes sense to call British.

Nobody in Newport, Shropshire, had a problem with Britishness. In Newport, Gwent, some of the Welsh felt British, though others preferred to call themselves European. But it was in Newport-on-Tay, near Dundee, that we found the greatest reluctance to sign up to a common identity of Britishness.

Here is Billy Kay, a local writer: 'The British identity that I'm supposed to feel part of I see as being first of all an imperial identity through the Empire and then an identity which has been forced by the idea of people coming together to fight two world wars. I don't think that's a healthy identity to carry into the 21st century.'

This is a common complaint – that Britishness is something from the past that has little relevance today. When the Act of Union was signed in 1707, people had to be persuaded to attach an extra loyalty to their long-standing allegiance to region or nation.

Successive governments used the common religion of Protestantism as a propaganda weapon to encourage the English, Scottish and Welsh to unite around a common flag – and against Catholic enemies.

The Empire – which was always the British, not the English Empire – was also a unifying force. It drew heavily on the expertise of the Scots and Welsh as doctors, traders, explorers and administrators.

Then there was the monarchy. Queen Victoria perhaps perfected the art of being monarch to all of Britain and the Empire. Meanwhile, successive wars have brought Britons together in defence of the Empire and the Union. It was the Battle of Britain, not the Battle of England, that took place over the Channel and southern counties.

But history is history: the Empire has gone, the Church no longer binds us, the Armed Forces are shrinking and the monarchy is troubled. Some people feel that the glue of nationhood has dried up. Alex Salmond, leader of the Scottish nationalists, no longer wants to be attached to what he sees as a Britain in decline. He looks to Europe as Scotland's new stage.

So do a surprising number in Newport, Gwent. Alan Richards, a sales director, has found that doing business with Europe has changed his outlook. 'I see our future very much as being linked to Europe as a whole: that includes England. I see England merely as part of Europe.'

The Times

B TOWNS AND CITIES, NORTH AND SOUTH

1 Here are the descriptions from a tourist guide book of some towns and cities in Britain.

Read the descriptions and add the names of six towns to the map.

Inverness

1 _____

Belfast

Scarborough

4 _____

5 _____

2 _____

Caernarvon

6 _____

Birmingham

Oxford

3 _____

Canterbury

NORWICH was one of the chief provincial cities of medieval England. When its walls were constructed (from 1197 to 1223), they enclosed almost a square mile, an area as big as that of the City of London. By that time it had become the capital of East Anglia. Its majestic cathedral and the narrow winding streets around it still remind the visitor of those ancient times.

LEEDS in West Yorkshire is a great commercial city, and its people are very proud of it. Some of the warehouses and factories which made it a wealthy city in the 18th and 19th centuries were destroyed some twenty to thirty years ago, but recently many have been renovated and developed for commercial or residential use. There are now many new buildings, as well as important historical buildings in the city centre.

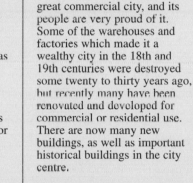

BRIGHTON is a seaside resort on the English Channel. Only 50 miles (80km) from London, it offers a good variety of lively entertainment. It is a cheerful place, bustling and crowded in the summer, but alive at every season of the year. Its royal pavilion is a masterpiece of eccentric English architecture.

DURHAM. Whatever travellers see or do not see in England, they must see this city, in the north east, just south of Newcastle upon Tyne. No one can forget the sight of its cathedral and castle rising together on a steep hill overlooking a loop in the River Wear, which almost surrounds them. The cathedral itself is one of the great medieval buildings of Europe.

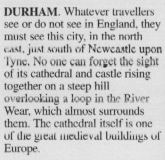

LIVERPOOL, a port in the north west of England, has a quality that is not found in quite the same way anywhere else in England: the quality of grandeur. Liverpool has this grandeur in its site on the broad Mersey river (more than half a mile wide) with the houses rising above it; in its great dock buildings, its broad streets, and its two enormous cathedrals.

EDINBURGH has long been the capital of Scotland. Edinburgh Castle is Edinburgh's principal building, dominating the city, perched on a rock over a hundred metres above sea level. Another important building is the Palace of Holyrood House, begun by James IV around 1500. In between the castle and the palace is the Royal Mile, which was the centre of Edinburgh life before the 17th century and is fascinating to visit now.

2 Now find these towns or cities on the map on page 7.

a The second city of Ireland and, since 1921, the capital of Northern Ireland. ....

b A busy little town in North Wales where for the first time in 1301 an English king's son was proclaimed Prince of Wales. ....

c A city in the south east of England, made famous by Chaucer's tales of medieval pilgrims. ....

d The most northerly town shown on the map, which is a centre for mountaineering and winter sports.

....

e England's second largest city, in the Midlands. It is larger than Manchester or Nottingham. ....

f About 80 km north west of London, this town in the south of England is the home of the country's oldest university.

....

g A small but well known seaside resort in the north east of England. ....

OPTION

1 Imagine that you are a travel agent in your country. What would be your advice for these situations:

   a A young person about to visit Britain wants a holiday by the sea with lots of things to do.

   b A history student would like to visit some interesting medieval buildings.

2 With a partner, imagine another tourist situation. Join another pair and take turns to role play:

   a people planning a visit to Britain.

   b travel agents advising them on things to see.

---

3 Discuss these two questions.

1 Think about your own country, and especially the part of it where you live.
What do you particularly like about it?

2 Are there important differences in your country between:
   – North and South?
   – East and West?
   – Capital city and rural areas?
Consider these possible differences.

     language; accent; dialects

     clothing; customs

     food

     the temperament or reputation of the people

     the climate

     class; education; social status

Join other students and compare your ideas. Write two or three key words
from your discussion on the board.

4 You are going to hear an interview with five young people.

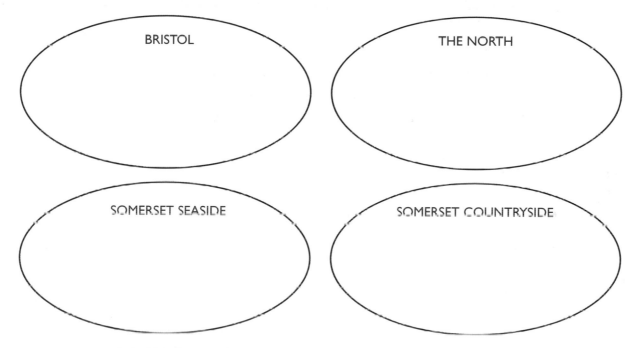 Listen and write where the students are from.

Anna from .... Sophie from ....

Will from .... Alex Turco from ....

Alex Ross from ....

5 The interviewer asks the five about the places they come from.

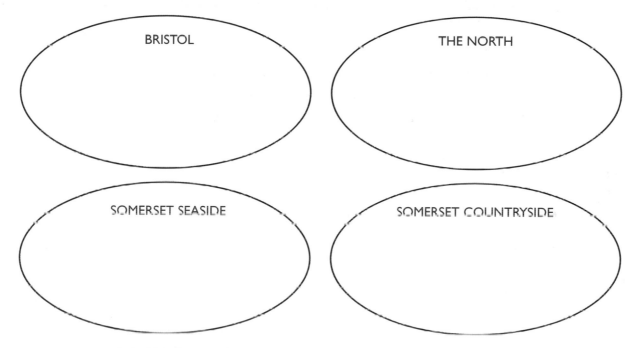 Listen and make notes.

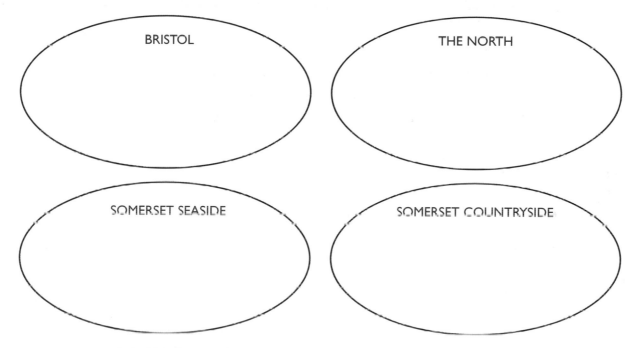

Listen again and add more details.

Compare your ideas about the place where you live with those of the English students.

6 Sophie talks about differences between the north and south in England.

Which category do you think these words go into?

	North or South?
affluent	
poor	
friendly	
loud	
restrained	
conservative	

 Listen and confirm your guesses.

7 The students talk about the differences between London and the rest of England.

Listen and write down key words. Prepare a summary of the students' ideas.

Join another student and present your summaries in turn.

C   ENGLISH HISTORY AND PLACE

1   What dates or events are meaningful in your country's history?
In small groups, discuss this question and agree on at least five events.
Next, decide on categories for your events. Are they

– military events, for example wars and battles?
– political, for example changes in systems of government?
– religious?
– events connected with the way people lived? the arts? the formation of the legal system? etc.

Write the events and their categories on the board.

2   Now look at the people and events from British history on the opposite page. Read the descriptions.
Discuss with a partner and choose five that you think are the most important (add others if you wish).
In small groups, compare your choices and say why you think they are important.

3   ▄▄ Listen to three English students giving their choices and reasons.
Complete the notes.

		Event	Reason
1	a	Roman invasion	Influence upon ....
	b	Henry VIII	The continued existence of the ....
	c	The	The troubles in ....
	d	....	Shows that war is ....
	e	....	Started a revolution of a different type.
2	a	....	Because all five are dates when Britain
	b	King Alfred defeats the Danes	....
	c	....	....
	d	The Battle of Waterloo	....
	e	....	
3	a	1215 the	The first hint of ....
	b	....	Gave the country ....
	c	....	Both stopped ....
	d	....	....
	e	....	The only time we've ever done it and we're very proud!

Did you make the same choices as the students? What do you think of their reasons?

1 The Roman invasion (AD 43) and occupation of Britain

For nearly four centuries the Romans made southern Britain a part of their empire. Much of the road system has a Roman origin. London, York, Chester, Bath and other important towns are built on Roman foundations. During the Roman occupation local government began, towns grew up along main roads, and agriculture was developed on large estates.

2 King Alfred defeats the Danes (AD 878)

When St Augustine arrived in England in AD 597, he brought Christianity and a new way of life. The Church acquired vast lands and wealth; its cathedrals and abbeys dominated the landscape; and the parish churches became the focal points of village life. The arts flourished, reaching a high point in the 8th century. The invasion of the Danes in the 9th century brought turmoil. It was not until the reign of Alfred the Great (871–99) that settled life could begin again. Alfred established an army and navy, divided the country into shires, and rebuilt the city of London.

3 The Battle of Hastings (William the Conqueror invades Britain, 1066)

An army of 60,000 men, commanded by Duke William of Normandy, landed in Sussex in 1066. In the battle of Hastings, Harold the English king was killed and William claimed England. The Bayeux tapestry tells the story of the Conquest. Norman French became the language of administration and justice, and had a lasting influence on the development of the English language.

4 Magna Carta (1215)

In response to the tyranny of King John (1199–1216), the noblemen of England drew up a document designed to limit the powers of the king and guarantee the rights of the people. The king met the barons at Runnymede, near Windsor, and was forced to sign this famous charter of personal and political liberty called Magna Carta.

5 Henry VIII and the founding of the Church of England (c. 1533)

In 1509 Henry VIII was crowned king. Eighteen years old, he was a keen sportsman and musician, and became the patron of the New Learning, the Renaissance. Henry created a separate Church of England, independent from Rome, and proclaimed himself its supreme head.

6 The Elizabethan age and Shakespeare

The reign of Elizabeth (1558–1603) was one of intellectual brilliance and immense commercial prosperity. William Shakespeare (1564–1616), born in Stratford-upon-Avon, is considered the greatest of the many playwrights of that age. Francis Drake and Walter Raleigh were two of the most famous Elizabethan explorers.

7 Declaration of independence by the Americans (1776)

Britain's attempt to impose taxes on the States of America to help finance its European wars led to a war of independence of 18 years between England and the United States. As a result, these large and valuable colonies separated from Britain and became an independent nation.

8 Union of Great Britain and Ireland (1800)

The success of the American colonies in throwing off the rule of England inspired unrest and open rebellion amongst the Irish, many of whom had long desired an independent republican state. The revolt was put down with great brutality and the Act of Union, which joined Ireland and Britain, set up a single legislative assembly for the two countries.

9 Battle of Waterloo (1815)

At the battle of Waterloo, fought in June 1815 near Brussels, Napoleon Bonaparte was defeated by a combination of Prussian, Belgian, Dutch and British troops, led by the Duke of Wellington and General Blücher. This put an end to Napoleon's military and political career.

10 Second World War (1939–1945)

The memory of the war remains strong in Britain even today. It was a time of great national solidarity in the face of threatened invasion and led to the founding of the European Union.

11 The Beatles' first albums (1960s)

The immense success of the group from Liverpool symbolised the vitality of Britain's popular culture and music.

12 Opening of the Channel Tunnel (1994)

The tunnel from England to France allows cars and passengers to cross the Channel in 20 minutes. It is important because it symbolises the country's increasing links with Continental Europe.

D LANGUAGES

1 Do you think these statements are True (✓) or False (✗)?

T   F

a In Britain you can hear a great variety of languages from many parts of the world. ◯ ◯

b There are many people who speak Welsh in Britain, but no broadcasts in Welsh. ◯ ◯

c Scots is the language of education and government in Scotland. ◯ ◯

d Scots is used in some newspapers in Scotland. ◯ ◯

e Gaelic is the official language of Northern Ireland. ◯ ◯

f The Isle of Man and Cornwall both have their own languages. ◯ ◯

2 Read the article and confirm your answers.

Spoken in the UK

Walk through any big British town and you can hear languages as diverse as Cantonese, Spanish, Urdu and Greek. But there are also a number of indigenous, or native, languages spoken within the UK.

According to the 1991 census, 527, 510 people said they spoke Welsh. It is increasingly used in schools and by some local authorities. Public pressure has led to more public services in Welsh. A Welsh television channel, S4C, began broadcasting in 1983 and there are radio stations and newspapers.

In some areas, the use of English in schools and in the media has contributed to the decline of minority languages. There were about 69,000 speakers of Gaelic in Scotland in 1991,

according to that year's census. The language, especially strong in the Outer Hebrides, is used in some schools but speakers have limited legal rights. It is not used in the courts, and it plays no part in the national government.

The Scots language, which is different from Scottish Gaelic, is so close a relative of English that it is often regarded as simply a northern dialect. It is spoken in the central belt of Scotland and the Lowlands. It was the everyday language here from the 14th century until the late 17th century. The upper classes slowly turned to English, influenced by the Union of the Crowns of England and Scotland in 1603. Most Scots speak a mixture of Scots and English, but English is the language of

education and the government.

There has been a Scots revival in recent years: the New Testament in Scots was published in 1985, and Scots is used in parts of the Scottish press.

There are speakers of the Irish Gaelic in Northern Ireland, but it has no official status there. Other native languages in Britain include Cornish in Cornwall and Manx Gaelic on the Isle of Man. The last native speaker of Cornish died in 1777 and the last speaker of Manx in 1974. There have been recent revivals, although the languages have no legal status.

The Guardian

3 Discuss these questions on language issues with the class.

Are all the languages and regional varieties equal in Britain? Does it matter which one you speak?

Which ones are taught in school and where?

Which ones can be heard in broadcasts?

Which ones can you use in court?

4 Discuss these questions about your country. Compare with Britain.

Is there one language only?

If so, is there a difference between its spoken and its written form?

If not, what is the status of the other languages?

5 Does the kind of English you speak affect your chances at a job interview? Here are seven varieties of English. Which do you think will be most likely to guarantee success at a job interview? Put them on the line.

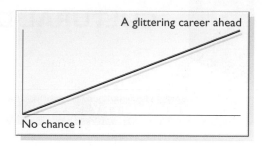

a a broad or 'thick' regional accent – e.g. *Scouse* (Liverpool), *Brummie* (Birmingham), *Cockney* (East London), *Glaswegian* (Glasgow)

b an educated Scottish accent

c an educated Welsh or Irish accent

d a 'posh' accent (upper class)

e a BBC voice – someone who sounds like a BBC announcer

f 'RP' – received pronunciation – a pronunciation that is widely accepted as correct

g an American or Australian accent

6 You are going to read an article on the relationship between accents and success in job interviews, published in *The Observer* (a Sunday newspaper). Which of the following opinions do you think the article might express?

a People with RP give the impression of being confident, intelligent and ambitious, even if they are not any of those things.

b People who have strong regional or non-standard accents are perceived as less friendly and less honest than RP people.

c The BBC uses announcers with 'standard' pronunciation because they will be more acceptable both at home and abroad.

d Accents from other countries are preferred because they are 'classless'.

e A woman who speaks RP is seen as more adventurous and feminine than one with a non-standard accent.

7 Read the article and compare its opinions and your choices.

Well-spoken Employees Wanted

It's no good just walking in and saying 'Gissa job' in thick Scouse, Brummie, or Glaswegian. If you want employment, get a 'proper accent' or you won't get past the first interview.

Don't be too posh, though – Oxford accents are off-putting and sounding like the Queen will only irritate your prospective employer, especially if you are a man.

The accent that will launch you on a glittering career is received pronunciation, or RP. This will give the impression that you are confident, intelligent and ambitious.

The ideal voice for getting that job is similar to a BBC announcer's voice, because 'It's pleasant to listen to', according to research by David Davey, a chartered psychologist specialising in executive assessment. The comparison did not please the BBC whose spokesman said: 'The BBC accent doesn't exist any more. We have an equal opportunities policy and any accent is acceptable provided that it is clearly understood.'

Standard accents are important in jobs that involve contact with customers with a wide range of accents, Mr Davey writes in the Institute of Personnel Management's journal, *Personnel Plus*. 'But for a research position, intelligence, education and experience would heavily outweigh even the worst Cockney or Scouse accent.'

There is consolation for those burdened with a strong accent: they are seen as friendlier, more generous, more honest and as having a better sense of humour than the RP brigade.

Mr Davey says that most educated Scottish accents rate highly, although below RP, of course. 'Educated' Welsh and Irish accents also score quite highly as do the mellower examples of English provincial brogues, such as those from Yorkshire and Tyneside.

American, Australian, South-African, Indian and West Indian accents might benefit from a certain 'classless' factor but all fail to challenge the supremacy of standard pronunciation.

RP women are thought to be more confident than women with 'non-standard accents', and they are also rated more highly in adventurousness, independence and femininity.

The Observer

CULTURAL DIVERSITY

A   A NEW COUNTRY

I Think of a country that is different from your own.
Imagine you are living there. In your new country,
you are looking out of the window: what can you see?

Make a simple poem by completing the lines.

  I look out of the window. I see ...

  The sky ...

Think about your life in the new country.

  People ...

  I'm getting used to ...

Now remember your life at home.

  Back home ...

  I miss ...

What are your feelings now?

  And so ...

2 Read your poem to a partner and talk about it.

3 With your partner, read a poem written by someone who came to live in England from another country.

ROLE 1	ROLE 2
Half the class: read 'Back Home' on page 21.	**Half the class: read 'Wherever I hang' on page 18.**

Where do you think the writers of the poems came from?
Are the feelings in your own poems similar to the poem you've read?
Are any of the details similar? Pick out at least two similarities.

....

....

....

....

....

4 Change partners. With someone who has read the other poem, compare your reactions.
Which poem do you prefer? Can you say why?

5 ▭▭ Listen to the two poems. What special things do the writers find difficult about life in England?
Is there anything they like?

6 Look at the following questions. Can you answer any of them?

a In the last fifty years, many people have come to live in Britain.
Do you know where some of these people came from? List a few countries.

b Can you think of possible reasons why people came to Britain?

c What did people in Britain think of the new 'ethnic minorities'?
('Ethnic minority' means people who came to Britain from abroad.)
Do you think they tried to stop people coming to Britain?

d Do you think there were any problems between native British people and immigrants?
Try to think of some examples.

e What proportion of the British population is now of 'ethnic' origin?
Do you think it's about: 6%, 12% or 24%?

Now turn the page and study the pictures and text.

B | NEW CITIZENS OF BRITAIN

About 8,000 West Indians were based in Britain as soldiers during the Second World War. Some of them decided to return to Britain after the war because of poor economic prospects at home. They were citizens of the British Empire, with the right to hold British passports and live and work in Britain. In fact many of them considered England as their 'mother country'.

In the 1950s and early 1960s, Britain had a strong economy and needed more workers. Many young Indians and Pakistanis came to Britain, where they could easily get jobs. Unlike the West Indians, Pakistanis and Indians never thought that they were moving to a 'mother country'. They moved for economic reasons.

In 1962 Britain passed a law, the Commonwealth Immigration Act, which meant that people from countries like Canada, Australia, India, Pakistan and Jamaica could no longer go and live in Britain unless they had a job there. Then in 1968 Britain passed a new Act. Now only people whose fathers or grandfathers were born in Britain were allowed to live there.

In 1965, the first Race Relations Act made racial discrimination a criminal offence, but it didn't cover housing or employment. Stronger Race Relations Acts were passed in 1968 and 1976. 'No Coloureds' and 'Europeans Only' signs were now illegal.

The third Race Relations Bill in 1976 was stronger and more extensive than previous ones. It set up the Commission for Racial Equality (CRE) to look into cases of discrimination on racial grounds.

Despite the laws against discrimination, there are still many inequalities. In proportion to their numbers, members of ethnic minorities still do more unskilled jobs, and make up a bigger share of the unemployed, than the majority of the population. But in education they now generally do better than others, and there is a growing number of politicians, lawyers, actors, writers, academics, musicians, business people and sports stars who provide models of successful lives in a multi-ethnic society.

Ethnic group	(Thousands)	% of total
White	52,936	93.6
Indian	925	1.6
Pakistani	587	1.0
Bangladeshi	209	1.4
Chinese	157	0.3
Other Asian	192	0.3
Black Caribbean	526	0.9
Black African	352	0.6
Black other (British, US, etc.)	132	0.2
Mixed	387	0.7
Other ethnic minorities	132	0.2
TOTAL	56,535	100

1 What details can you add to the answers you gave to the five questions on page 15? Discuss the questions with others in the class.

2 🔲🔲 On the cassette you will hear an interview with an Indian family who came to live in England in 1965. Listen to the cassette and answer these questions.

Part A (Mother)

1 What surprised her when she first arrived in England?
2 What does she miss most about India?
3 What work does she do?

Part B (Father)

1 What difficulties did he face when he started work?
2 How did he help other Indians?

Part C (Son)

1 Does he feel he is Indian or English?
2 How does he feel different from his English friends?
3 What is his experience of racism?

3 Read this extract from the novel *Second Class Citizen* by the Nigerian writer, Buchi Emecheta. Find at least one way in which the experience of the narrator is similar to the mother's experience you heard on the tape.

The house was grey with green windows. She could not tell where the house began and where it ended, because it was joined to other houses in the street. She had never seen houses like that before, joined together like that. In Lagos houses were usually completely detached with the yards on both sides, the compound at the back and verandas in front. These ones had none of those things. They were long solid blocks, with doors opening into the street. The windows were arranged in straight rows along the streets. On looking round, Adah noticed that one could tell which windows belonged to which door by the colour the frames were painted. Most of the houses seemed to have the same curtains for their windows.

'They all look like churches, you know; monasteries,' Adah remarked.

'They build their houses like that here because land is not as plentiful as it is in Lagos. I am sure that builders of the future will start building houses like that when Nigeria is fully industrialized. At the moment we can afford to waste land in building spacious verandas and back yards.'

'We may never be as bad as this. Jammed against each other.'

Francis did not make any comment. There was no need. He opened the door into what looked to Adah like a tunnel. But it was a hall; a hall with flowered walls! It was narrow and it seemed at first as if there were no windows. Adah clutched at Titi, and she in turn held her mother in fear. They climbed stairs upon stairs until they seemed to be approaching the roof of the house. Then Francis opened one door and showed them into a room, or a half-room. It was very small with a single bed at one end and a new settee which Francis had bought with the money Adah had sent him to buy a top coat with. The space between the settee and the bed was just enough for a Formica-topped table, the type she had had in the kitchen in Lagos.

'Are we going to live here?' she managed to ask.

'Well, I know you will not like it, but this is the best I can do. You see, accommodation is very short in London, especially for black people with children. Everybody is coming to London. The West Indians, the Pakistanis and even the Indians, so that African students are usually grouped together with them. We are all blacks, all coloureds, and the only houses we can get are horrors like these.'

Well, what could she say? She simply stared. She said nothing even when she learned that the toilet was outside, four flights of stairs down, in the yard; nor when she learned that there was no bath and no kitchen. She swallowed it all, just like a nasty pill.

4 What are the main things which surprise or shock the narrator about conditions in England, especially English housing? How do conditions in England compare with those in Nigeria?

C 'THAT'S MY HOME'

Wherever I hang

I leave me people, me land, me home
For reasons, I not too sure
I forsake de sun
And de humming-bird splendour
Had big rats in de floorboard
So I pick up me new-world-self
And come, to this place call England
At first I feeling like I in dream –
De misty greyness
I touching de walls to see if they real
They solid to de seam
And de people pouring from de underground system
Like beans
And when I look up to de sky
I see Lord Nelson high – too high to lie

And is so I sending home photos of myself
Among de pigeons and de snow
And is so I warding off de cold
And is so, little by little
I begin to change my calypso ways
Never visiting nobody
Before giving them clear warning
And waiting me turn in queue
Now, after all this time
I get accustom to de English life
But I still miss back-home side
To tell you de truth
I don't know really where I belaang

    Yes, divided to de ocean
    Divided to de bone

Wherever I hang me knickers – that's my home.

Grace Nichols

Trevor McDonald
Television newsreader

Diane Abbott
Member of Parliament

Prince Naseem
Boxer

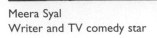

Meera Syal
Writer and TV comedy star

1 What is life like now for the ethnic minorities of Britain? Look at the texts below, and make notes under two headings:

Positive aspects

....

....

....

....

....

Negative aspects

....

....

....

....

....

1 A coloured person has to be twice as good as an Englishman for the same job.

Dilip Hiro,
Black British, White British

2 In the 50 years since the first Asian influx to Britain, Asians have moved on from the old stereotyped image of the struggling corner-shop businessman. There are now more than 300 Asian millionaires in Britain.

The Independent

3 The immaculate condition, inside and out, of many Italian houses is a noticeable aspect of many areas of English towns ... Sheds and garages are used for making and storing wine, gardens are used for growing vegetables rather than flowers, colourful but well maintained paintwork on window and door frames is preferred ... and finally in the larger Italian communities where there are Italian bakeries a shopping bag can often be seen hanging from a back or side door. Delivery of a large loaf of Italian bread is made early in the morning by way of the shopping bag.

Terri Colpi,
The Italian Factor

4 Black people are more likely than their white counterparts to be stopped by the police. If stopped, they are more likely to be arrested. If arrested, they are more likely to be charged. If charged, they are more likely to be remanded in custody; and if convicted, they are more likely to receive a sentence of imprisonment.

The Director of the Prison Reform Trust

5 Those of us who live here gain the advantages of both Asian and Western cultures. We have the strength that comes from our culture and religions, and from our families. Although the extended family exists less and less in its traditional form, family bonds do remain very strong. But we also have the educational and career opportunities that the West offers.

Kamlesh Bahl, Equal Opportunities Commission

6 Progress has been made in race relations in the last few years and there are many optimistic signs. There's a growing young, articulate, black middle class. Black Britons born here have a confidence that their parents never possessed. Their educational achievements are beginning to foster a benign cycle of upward mobility. It's the employment picture, however, that's still depressing ... While unemployment among white people is 8%, among ethnic minorities it's 15%.

The Guardian

7 In Britain one is forced to be constantly aware of colour, even when you tell yourself you don't care and that you're damned if you're going to live your life by other people's precepts. But the collective consciousness isn't so easily dismissed, unless you live the life of a hermit. As long as you live in society the collective won't let you alone.

Adewale Maja-Pearce,
How Many Miles To Babylon?

2 What do you think: do the positive aspects outweigh the negative? What did you find most interesting in the texts? Compare and discuss your ideas.

D CULTURAL CONFLICT

1 It's important to remember that people from all over the world – not just
Africa, Asia and the Caribbean – have been immigrants to Britain in the
past 50 years. The last Census shows, for instance, that more than 175,000
people living in Britain were born in Australia, New Zealand or Canada;
74,000 in Poland, 78,000 in Cyprus, 91,000 in Italy, 143,000 in the USA,
215,000 in Germany, and nearly 600,000 in the Republic of Ireland. Some
have come to Britain as political refugees; others for economic or career
opportunities. Every immigrant community has its own story, its own ways
of adapting to the stresses and challenges of life in a new country.

There are sometimes cultural conflicts. Here are two examples.

In the early 1980s, a considerable controversy developed
between the Italians in Bedford and the Town Council.
According to the Council, the Italians were turning the
graves of their relatives into 'gardens', which is against
cemetery policy. The tradition of the Italians in Britain is to
delimit the grave, perhaps with a little fence, and to 'grow'
rather than 'place' flowers. In 1982 the Bedfordshire Times
carried a front-page article with the title 'Relatives Fight to
Honour Dead'... Many of the Italians in question were
indeed prepared to 'fight' and go to prison over the issue.

Terri Colpi, *The Italian Factor*

The private Islamia School in London
campaigned for 10 years to become the
first state-aided Muslim school
in Britain. In August 1993 the
application was refused by the
Government because there were 'too
many surplus places' in schools nearby.
Yet only two weeks earlier the
Government had given state aid
to another primary school in the area.
The school's leading supporter, Yusuf
Islam (formerly the singer Cat Stevens),
described the decision as 'an outrage'.
He pointed out that there were 4,100
state-aided Christian schools, 21 for
Jews, but none for Britain's 1 million
Muslims. In 1998 the Islamia School's
application for state aid was accepted.

Based on reports in
The Times Educational Supplement

2 Choose one of these examples and decide how you would settle the argument.
List reasons both for and against your decision, and compare with others in the class.

3 Find an example of a recent cultural conflict in your country and describe the arguments on each
side. You can do this in the form of a newspaper report, a poster, a mini-drama, or a TV
documentary.

An Italian festival in Bedford

The Islamia school, London

Back Home

Back home
    the sun does greet you with a smile
    creep up the bedclothes until
    you open your eye
    Bright and hot
    The sky blue and clear
    Every day does fill you with cheer

Back home
    is all type of mango
    banana, orange and plum
    growing in we garden
    ripening in the heat
    Any time you want you can
    pick some and eat

Back home
    the sea at we back door
    I could step out the house
    and run down to bathe
    listen to the waves when I in bed
    They does soothe me good
    They does help me sleep

Back home
    But I not back home
    I here in England
    where the sun not so hot
    and the fruit not so ripe
    and the sea does chill your feet

Back home
    is just a sad-sweet memory

                Amryl Johnson

A   SPORTS THROUGH THE AGES

1   How many names of sports can you think of in English? Write down as many as you can in three minutes.

2   Sports are often grouped into categories. Here are some of the most common.

water sports	indoor sports	winter sports	motor sports
target sports	equestrian sports	racquet sports	ball games

Some sports may go in more than one category. Tennis, for instance, is both a *racquet sport* and a *ball game*.

Look at the list of sports you made in Exercise 1, and sort them into categories. Write them on the board.

3   ▭▭ Listen to the interviews with four British people – Jacqui, Andrew, Richard and Wendy – and guess what their favourite sports are from the clues they give. Fill in the table.

Name	Clues	Sport
Jacqui		
Andrew		
Richard		
Wendy		

4   With a partner, look at these questions about the history of sport. Answer them if you can, making guesses where you are not sure.

a Is sport in the 20th century different from the past? In what ways?

b Do you think there were sports professionals before the 20th century? In what sports?

c Was the most important period for the development of modern sports the 5th century BC, the 16th century, the 18th century, or the 19th century?

d Which modern sports originated in Britain?

e Did governments always encourage people to take part in sports? Why or why not?

f What problems did women have in playing sports in the 19th century?

5 Check your answers by reading the article below. Write down the exact words used in the article that give you the answers.

From the 14th century a wide variety of sports and games became common in Europe. From that time the growth was steady. It is also noticeable that there were a number of edicts and statutes (for the most part ineffectual) forbidding the pursuit of certain sporting activities. These were made because rulers feared they might divert men from remaining in a state of readiness for war by taking regular archery practice and other forms of military training.

During the latter part of the 16th and during the 17th and 18th centuries sports and games became increasingly popular and there are numerous records available for a study of their history. However, the second half of the 19th century is the period of development. Much of it was achieved in England and in Britain. In fact from the late Middle Ages up to, say, the 1930s the British contribution to sport is without parallel. Among the sports that originated in Britain are football, rugby, badminton, croquet, lawn tennis, cricket, squash, snooker and table tennis.

In the 20th century a number of sports and games have become highly professional. With professionalism have come more intense competition, better standards of performance and greater financial rewards. In Classical times professionalism was established for centuries, especially among boxers, wrestlers, jockeys, athletes and chariot drivers. However, by the middle of the 5th century AD it had died out in sport and was not revived until the 16th century ...

There were signs of modern professionalism in England in the 18th century, in which period we find, for example, professional boxers and cricketers. In the closing years of the 19th century association football and Rugby League football became professional and there were an increasing number of professional golfers and cricketers by the turn of the century. Since then professionalism has become typical of many sports and games ...

At the higher levels sportsmen and women are more committed and dedicated than ever before, and today it scarcely seems credible that at the 1896 Olympic Games in Athens some of the athletes who took part were visitors who happened to be in the city at the time. Now, performers prepare themselves with the utmost assiduousness for every event. Performances are analysed on film and video tape. Teams have 'clinics' before and after matches.

Many people think that sport has become too serious and it may well be argued that when the desire and will to win over-ride all other considerations then a form of futility has set in. What is one to make of that celebrated remark by Vince Lombardi, the great American football coach, that 'Winning isn't everything, it's the only thing'? At the other end of the value scale we have the traditions in West Sumatra where non-achievement was the desirable goal. A man who came first in a race might well be banned from taking part again! ...

A very important development since about 1900 has been the ever-increasing participation of women in many sports and games. In ancient Greece women were allowed to compete in athletic contests and towards the end of the pre-Christian era, when women were becoming more emancipated (especially in the cities), there were more and more athletic events for them. From that period until the 19th century there is little mention of women being much involved in sport, though it was perfectly acceptable for queens and noblewomen to hunt and use falcons. In the 18th century male attitudes towards female participation became more sympathetic and it is perhaps a little surprising to reflect that women's cricket was tolerably well established in England by the 1760s. However, it is not until the last 25 years of the 19th century that we find women (nearly always of the middle and upper classes) taking part in a variety of open-air sports; notably, lawn tennis, badminton, hockey, golf, skating, archery, baseball (or rounders) and some others. Victorian fashions were of course a problem. Movement was restricted and many men felt that sporting activities were unbecoming for women. Female emancipation and determination triumphed and women were soon taking part in the Olympic Games. Basketball, netball, volleyball, gymnastics, skiing, fencing, swimming, and equestrian sports (besides those sports already mentioned) became regular activities for women. Fears that sport was incompatible with femininity proved illusory.

J. A. Cuddon, *The Macmillan Dictionary of Sport and Games*

6 Write down one fact from the article that you found most interesting or surprising. Compare with others in the class.

7 Prepare a mini-debate in your class, on one of these themes:

'Sport should be a form of play, not a way of earning money.'
'Winning isn't everything, it's the only thing.'

8 Project. Choose a sport you enjoy. Research and write a short history of it, and present it in the form of a poster.

B | THE SPORTING CALENDAR

1 Read this passage about sporting events in Britain.

> A number of sporting events in Britain are national institutions. Some are popular occasions, attended by thousands of spectators from all levels of society and watched on television by millions. Others are elegant and exclusive outdoor parties for the rich and their friends, where sport is secondary to social enjoyment. The Cup Final is an example of one extreme, Ascot of the other. Some, such as Wimbledon, are an interesting mixture of both.
>
> Most of these events are attended by members of the Royal Family as well as by politicians, film stars, singers and business people. The venues are equipped with luxurious 'hospitality suites', used by companies to promote their business and thank important clients for their loyalty. Tickets for most of these events can be expensive, but not usually beyond the reach of ordinary people. They are often hard to find, however, as space is limited and there is great demand.
>
> There are, of course, hundreds more events which draw large crowds – notably in football, cricket, golf, sailing and motor-racing – and everyone has their favourites. The historical traditions, the holiday atmosphere, and the pleasure and excitement of the spectators (often with an element of suspense provided by the weather) make these some of the most enjoyable and friendly occasions of the year.

2 Find a word or expression which means:

a the place where a sporting event happens
b people who watch a sporting event
c not open to everybody, restricted
d too expensive for
e many people want it

3 Describe one of your country's main sporting events. Where and when does it take place? When was it first held? Who takes part? What is it like to watch?

Henley Regatta

4 Imagine you are going on a visit to Britain and planning to see some sport. Role play a visit to a travel agent – you have card 1, and your partner has card 4. Then change roles – your partner has card 3, you have card 2.

FA Cup Final

Frith, *Derby Day*, 1856–8

ROLE CARD 1

Next year (between January and May), you are planning a trip with friends to Britain. Find out:
- is there a classic horse-race that you can see? Where and when is it? What kind of race is it?
- is there any international rugby? Which teams are playing? For which trophies?
- is there anything for your friends (one is a rowing fanatic, the other a keen football fan)?

Find out some details of dates, venues, etc.

ROLE CARD 2

You are a travel agent. Your partner is a customer. Read the text on this card, look carefully at the pictures, and answer your partner's questions.

By May the cricket season is already under way, with village and pub sides playing at weekends and the professional teams (all representing counties, such as Lancashire, Essex and Glamorgan) playing matches throughout the week. From June to August a series of international matches, known as 'Test Matches', are played between England and a visiting national team from another country where cricket is professionally played: Australia, India, New Zealand, Pakistan, South Africa, Sri Lanka, the West Indies, Zimbabwe. The first Test Match was between England and Australia at Melbourne in 1877. The matches last five days, and are played at various county cricket grounds around England, including Lord's – 'the home of cricket' in St John's Wood, London. Lord's is the headquarters of the historic Marylebone Cricket Club (MCC), founded in 1787, which formulated the rules of cricket. The Lord's Test in June is one of the high points of the English summer.

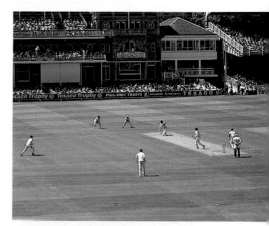

Test Match at Lord's

June is the height of the flat-racing season (horse races on flat courses, without jumps). The most fashionable and exclusive sporting event of the year is Royal Ascot, a four-day race meeting at Ascot Heath near Windsor in Berkshire, first held under Queen Anne in 1711. Ascot is traditionally attended by the monarch, whose horses compete in the races. Newspapers, society magazines and TV always show pictures of the smartest and most extravagantly dressed spectators: in fact the human beings compete just as much as the horses.

The first Saturday in June is Derby Day. The Derby is a 2.4 km race which has been held at Epsom Downs race-course, south of London, since 1780. This is a more popular event than Ascot. Its chaotic and vibrant holiday atmosphere was vividly captured by the Victorian painter William Powell Frith (*Derby Day*, 1856–8). 'I have more fun there than at any other race I know', wrote the American journalist A. J. Liebling.

Royal Ascot

At the end of June is the All-England Championships in lawn tennis, better known as Wimbledon. This two-week event is one of the major international tennis competitions and part of the Grand Slam series. It attracts 250,000 spectators each year, with millions more watching on TV. The first Championship was held on a croquet lawn at the All-England Croquet and Lawn Tennis Club in the south London suburb of Wimbledon in 1877. The atmosphere is genteel rather than rowdy. Part of the tradition of Wimbledon is the sale of strawberries and cream to the crowds, and the rain which regularly interrupts play.

At the start of July is the Henley Royal Regatta, founded in 1839. This is held over four days at Henley-on-Thames in Oxfordshire. Officially an international rowing competition with many handsome silver trophies to be won, it is also a major social event where ladies in summer dresses and men in blazers and rowing caps stroll along the banks of the river, or cruise up and down in smart motor-boats, partying and drinking champagne. There is an air of carefree gaiety that suggests the Edwardian age (1901–10) when river-boating was at its most popular.

Wimbledon

ROLE CARD 3

Next year (between May and September), you are planning a trip with friends to Britain. Find out:
- is there an occasion when you can be sure to see the Queen? What kind of clothes should you wear?
- where can you go to watch cricket? Decide if you want to see a big international match or a local game.
- what would make a good sporting day outside London in June or July? Get as much information as you can.
- is there anything for your friend who loves watching tennis?

Ask for details of dates, etc.

ROLE CARD 4

You are a travel agent. Your partner is a customer. Read the text on this card, look carefully at the pictures, and answer your partner's questions.

The Grand National

The first major sporting event of the year is the Five Nations Championship, played since 1910 between the national rugby football teams of England, Scotland, Wales, Ireland and France. This takes place over five Saturdays between January and March, with matches at Twickenham (in London), Murrayfield (Edinburgh), Arms Park (Cardiff), Lansdowne Road (Dublin) and Parc des Princes (Paris). Fans of each side travel to support their team, and the atmosphere in a city on the night before a match is full of excitement and high spirits. There are no trophies for this championship, only the honour of winning the Grand Slam (defeating all opponents) or, among the British teams, the Triple Crown. In 1998 Italy was invited to join the championship – making it Six Nations from January 2000.

The Boat Race, between Oxford and Cambridge Universities, is held on the last Saturday of March from Putney to Mortlake on the River Thames in West London. Although this is an amateur contest, it is physically very demanding: the course is almost 7km, the crews train hard under professional coaches, and the competition is intense. There are no tickets for the Boat Race – anyone can go and watch from the river banks and the bridges over the Thames, and enjoy the scenes of festivity and foolery that accompany it. The first boat race was in 1829.

The Five Nations Championship

Also in March is the Grand National, a horse race held every year at Aintree in Liverpool since 1839. This is the most popular race in Britain, and millions of pounds are taken in bets. The course is long (over 7 km) and very hazardous. There are 30 jumps – high wooden fences and ditches filled with water – and horses and jockeys frequently fall. Perhaps because of the risks and exceptional physical demands, horses that win the Grand National – such as Red Rum, which won in 1973, 1974 and 1977 – often become popular heroes.

The football season ends in May with the FA Cup Final ('FA' stands for Football Association). The FA Cup Final is played at Wembley, the English national stadium, and the winners' trophy and medals are traditionally presented by the King or Queen. Unlike the Football League, the FA Cup is a knockout competition open to all football clubs in England. Five hundred clubs take part, and it offers the excitement of little-known teams playing (and sometimes beating) famous clubs like Arsenal or Manchester United. The Cup Final, like the Grand National, is immensely popular. It was first held in 1872. There is also a Scottish Cup Final, at the national stadium of Hampden Park, which was first played in 1874.

The University Boat Race, 1871

5 Design a sporting calendar for the year in Britain.

C   LIKES AND DISLIKES

1 Active participation in sport is very popular in Britain, and is encouraged from the earliest years of school. Local authorities are obliged by law to provide sports facilities for the public, and there are hundreds of sports clubs all over the country.

Here is a list of the 20 most popular sports played by 11- to 19-year-olds in Britain. With a partner, choose what you think are the *ten most popular*.

aerobics	horse riding	athletics	ice skating
badminton	netball	basketball	roller skating
billiards/snooker	rounders	cricket	rugby
cycling	swimming	football	table tennis
gymnastics	ten pin bowling	hockey	tennis

Now choose the top five. Check your guesses on page 92.

2 Which are the top five sports in your country? And among your friends? Are these different from British choices? Why do you think this is?

3 Look at the list of words below. For each one, write down a synonym (a word with the same meaning) and an antonym (a word with the opposite meaning). Use a dictionary if you need to. If you can't find a single word, use a phrase. The first two are done for you.

Words	*Synonyms*	*Antonyms*
honourable	decent, honest, fair	dishonourable
boring	dull, tedious	exciting, lively
generous		
keen		
unselfish		
free		
moral		
decent		
sordid		
happy		
boastful		
fair play		
violence		
pleasure		
hatred		
terror		
jealousy		

4 Which of the words in Exercise 3 do
you associate with sport? Make a word net.

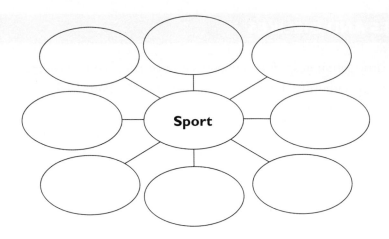

5 In English, the ideas of *sport* and *good behaviour* are often connected. For example, ideas of justice,
generosity and respect for the rights of others are expressed in terms such as 'fair play',
'sportsmanship' and 'playing the game'. A person who works well with other people is often
referred to as 'a good team player'. Bad behaviour of many kinds can be described as 'unsporting',
'not playing the game' or even 'not cricket'. These connections between sport and good behaviour
were established in Victorian Britain, particularly in schools, where sport was seen as a way of
developing courage, leadership, unselfishness and other social virtues.

Are there similar connections and expressions in your language? Make a list of phrases you use to
describe good and bad behaviour.

6 Here are some opinions, both for and against this idea of sportsmanship. Read them, then try to
find a place for each one on the diagram on the opposite page. The first one (A) is done for you as
an example. The author claims a very high moral value for cricket, and implies that he enjoys the
game too, so A is placed high up and to the right. Now mark the other quotations on the diagram
according to where you think they should go.

A *'You do well to love it [cricket], for it is more free from
anything sordid, anything dishonourable, than any
game in the world. To play it keenly, honourably,
generously, self-sacrificingly is a moral lesson in
itself, and the class-room is God's air and sunshine.'*
Lord Harris, cricket enthusiast

B *'I have practically never played football
or cricket, for which I am profoundly
thankful. Even to watch these games is
for me an anguish of boredom.'*
Malcolm Muggeridge, journalist and humorist

C *'Football makes millions of people
happy every day.'*
Ian Wright, England footballer

D *'Serious sport has nothing to do with fair
play. It is bound up with hatred,
jealousy, boastfulness, disregard of all
rules and sadistic pleasure in witnessing
violence: in other words it is war minus
the shooting.'*
George Orwell, novelist and essayist

E *'Having a bad head for heights myself, I trained myself deliberately and painfully to overcome it. We used to go climbing in the turrets and towers of Harlech Castle. I have worked hard on myself defining and dispersing my terrors. The simple fear of heights was the first to be overcome.'*

Robert Graves, poet

F *'I teach sportsmanship according to the British Idea. I teach that decent behaviour wins in the end as a natural order of things.'*

Captain W. E. Johns, boys' adventure story writer

G *'If you spend a lot of time on sportsmanship, you're going to spend a lot of time losing.'*

Glenn Dobbs, US sports coach

H *'I love soccer because it is vital and fluid, and free from the little legal barriers that frustrate the rest of our everyday activities.'*

Danny Blanchflower, England footballer

I *'Football, in itself, is a grand game for developing a lad physically and also morally, for he learns to play with good temper and unselfishness, to play in his place and "play the game", and these are the best training for any game of life.'*

Robert Baden-Powell, founder of the boy scout movement

pleasure

Ⓐ

negative moral value

positive moral value

suffering

7 Choose one of these opinions that you agree with, and another that you disagree with.
Write a dialogue between two people who hold these views, or a short defence of your view.

D   FOOTBALL: FANS AND PLAYERS

1 Read the notes about recent changes in professional football in Britain. Tick the columns to show whether similar changes have happened in your country.

		Similar?	Different?
a	Major football clubs have become highly successful businesses with huge budgets made possible by advertising, sponsorship and television fees.	◯	◯
b	A large number of famous international players and managers now work for British clubs, and have raised the level of skill and spectacle in British games.	◯	◯
c	Spectators now have to sit down in football stadiums (most used to stand on 'terraces'), and prices are much higher than before.	◯	◯
d	Going to football matches is no longer an all-male pursuit. It is now seen as entertainment for the whole family – mothers and daughters included. It has also become more middle-class.	◯	◯
e	Crowd violence and hooliganism at football matches is declining, partly because of the changes outlined above.	◯	◯
f	Since 1992, when *Fever Pitch*, a book by Nick Hornby, became a bestseller, football has become a fashionable subject for writers.	◯	◯

Compare your answers with others in your class.

2 Think of a sporting event you went to as a child. What sport was it? Where did you sit or stand? Who did you go with? What was the weather like? Do you remember what you wore? Or what you ate? Or what anyone said? What feelings did you have? Make some notes and tell a partner about it.

3 Complete these sentences, using your own ideas.

If I have a choice between watching and playing a sport, I choose ...., because ....

When I watch professional sportsmen I feel .... because they ....

I think a great team is the result of ....

Supporting a football club is ....

I think professional footballers earn .... money. The effect of this is ....

4 Read the two passages about football fans. One is by a player, the other by a fan.
As you read, make notes under four headings:

Criticism of fans	*Defence of fans*	*Criticism of players*	*Defence of players*
....	....	....	....
....	....	....	....
....	....	....	....
....	....	....	....
....	....	....	....

The first passage is from *Mr Wright*, the autobiography of England footballer Ian Wright. In 1996, Wright was playing for Arsenal, one of the best-known clubs in Britain, based in North London. He had previously played for a smaller club, Crystal Palace, in South London. Whenever Wright played for Arsenal against his old team, the fans called him a traitor. Here he explains how he feels about such accusations:

When I think of the stick I get now from Palace fans, it makes me wonder about their mentality ... Fans want it all their way every time. Of course they want the best players to stay at the club, but then after five or six good years of service, they cannot respect that a player wants to better himself in his playing standards and financially. It's crazy: none of the values of real life matter where fans are concerned. Tell me, if somebody was offered a better job, with a company car and a massive wage rise plus an extra week's holiday and BUPA, would they turn it down? No, they'd be mugs to, so why should a footballer be any different? I love the passion and enthusiasm and love that fans bring to the game, but sometimes it's a hell of a job trying to make them see sense.

The second passage is from *Fever Pitch* by Nick Hornby, which describes the life and passions of a dedicated Arsenal supporter.

One thing I know for sure about being a fan is this: it is not a vicarious pleasure, despite all appearances to the contrary, and those who say they would rather do than watch are missing the point. ... When there is some kind of triumph, the pleasure does not radiate from the players outwards until it reaches the likes of us at the back of the terraces in a pale and diminished form; our fun is not a watery version of the team's fun, even though they are the ones that get to score the goals and climb the steps at Wembley to meet Princess Diana. The joy we feel on occasions like this is not a celebration of others' good fortune, but a celebration of our own; and when there is a disastrous defeat the sorrow that engulfs us is, in effect, self-pity, and anyone who wishes to understand how football is consumed must realise this above all things. The players are merely our representatives, chosen by the manager rather than elected by us, but our representatives nonetheless, and sometimes if you look hard you can see the little poles that join them together, and the handles at the side that enable us to move them. I am a part of the club, just as the club is a part of me; and I say this fully aware that the club exploits me, disregards my views, and treats me shoddily on occasions, so my feeling of organic connection is not built on a muddle-headed and sentimental misunderstanding of how professional football works. This Wembley win [against Liverpool in the final of the Littlewoods Cup, in 1987] belonged to me every bit as much as it belonged to the players, and I worked every bit as hard for it as they did. The only difference between me and them is that I have put in more hours, more years, more decades than them, and so had a better understanding of the afternoon, a sweeter appreciation of why the sun still shines when I remember it.

5 Which passage says more about money?
Which says more about feelings?
Which do you agree with?
Is there anything in either passage which would *not* be true of footballers or fans in your country?

A THE TRADITIONAL FOODS OF BRITAIN

1 Look at this restaurant menu. Which of these dishes come from Britain? Do you know where the others come from?

2 Make a list of typical dishes from your country. Do they have any features in common (similar ingredients, cooking methods, etc.)?
What about the British dishes from the menu?
Do they have any features in common?

3 Can you name the foods in the picture?
(Some are in the menu.)

Starters
Melon with Parma ham
Smoked salmon
Vegetable samosas
Kipper pâté with toast
Taramasalata
Oxtail soup

Main courses

Seafood
Deep fried cod or haddock and chips
Herrings in oatmeal with mustard sauce
Paella
Fisherman's pie
Curried prawns with pilau rice
Moules marinière

Meat
Beef goulash
Roast sirloin of beef with Yorkshire pudding
Steak and kidney pie
Shish kebab
Spare ribs Tex-Mex style
Peking duck
Wiener schnitzel
Roast pheasant with bread sauce
Osso buco

Desserts
Apple and blackberry crumble
Crème caramel
Apple strudel
Rhubarb pie and custard
Treacle sponge pudding

4 What experience do you have of food in Britain? Do you think people eat well or badly? Choose some appropriate words from the list below, and add some of your own.

exciting	dull
cheap	expensive
tasty	bland
well-prepared	poorly prepared
international	traditional
surprising	predictable

5 Here are some comments on the quality of British food – some positive, some negative. Place each one on this scale.

Very good · · · · · · · · · Mixed good and bad · · · · · · · · · Very bad

A

We Britons are internationally famous for our gardens, our dogs, our beer, our cloth, our cars, our villages, our whisky, our public schools, our monarchy, our democratic institutions, our cricket – umpteen books have been written explaining their glories to those unfortunate enough to have been born outside these islands. But nobody has yet written a book about the bad food for which we are equally famous overseas.

Derek Cooper,
The Bad Food Guide

B

Sausage ... even the word has a sizzling, succulent sound, and what memories it evokes. It could form the framework for an autobiography, starting with sausages for breakfast on Sunday, which is one of the first things I can remember. Then, during World War I, when I was about four years old and living in Hampshire, my grandparents provided refuge for a displaced Belgian family. Monsieur Schoof was a *charcutier* and he soon found a job with a butcher in the nearest town. On his first free day he bicycled eight miles simply to tell us that on no account were we to consider buying sausages from the shop in which he worked. They were a travesty ... the ingredients utterly deplorable ... the abysmal ignorance of his master beyond comprehension ... etc. etc. At that age I was amazed that sausages could arouse such vehement passions in a man.

Antony and Araminta Hippisley Coxe,
Book of Sausages

C

In England, especially in the big towns, fish and chips and hamburgers have gradually replaced the traditional lamb and mint sauce, while an impressive arsenal of sweets and snacks takes care of those 'peckish' moments between meals. Bad eating habits start very young: chemists sell pots of spaghetti with bolognese sauce for babies, and you often see one-year-olds with hamburgers in their mouths.

Yet for many Britons, *Sunday lunch* remains sacred: British families still enjoy their famous *roast beef* or *roast pork*, accompanied by the traditional *Yorkshire pudding* (a kind of soufflé), not forgetting *roast potatoes* of course, and perhaps some peas, green beans or, in winter, brussels sprouts.

Guide Bleu: Grande Bretagne –
(translated from the French)

D

The idea that the Puritans with their miserable diet of pickled herrings had any permanent influence on English cooking is as false as the French delusion that we only had one sauce. In the early eighteenth century we ate more and we ate better than people in the rest of Europe. Travellers said that nowhere else could you find such tender juicy steaks, such luscious thick-cut mutton chops and huge prime cuts of beef done to a turn on spit or gridiron. Our pies were famous and the cooking in our taverns and chop houses was renowned throughout Europe.

Sheila Hutchins, *English Recipes*

6 Using Text A or B as a model, write one of the following.

   a A sentence about your country, beginning, 'We .... are internationally famous for ...., but ....'

   b Your most vivid childhood memory of food.

"All right, who'd like a jacket potato?"

7 Some famous British dishes have strange or surprising names. ('Welsh rabbit', for instance, contains no rabbit at all. It is made with bread, beer, mustard and cheese.)
Look at these definitions of another well-known dish, 'toad in the hole'. Which is the right one?

   a Stewed plums in a rich vanilla custard.

   b A country pie made with frog's legs, mushrooms and cream.

   c Sausages baked in Yorkshire pudding batter.

8 Here are some more curious dishes for you to use in a game of 'Call My Bluff'.
Divide into teams of three. Your teacher will give you the correct definition of one dish.
Make up two false definitions of the dish. Read these out, together with the
correct definition, to the opposing team. If they guess which is the right
one, they score a point. If they guess wrong, you score a point.

Jugged hare	Spotted dog
Shepherd's pie	Lancashire hotpot
Haggis wi' neeps and tatties	Bangers and mash
Bubble and squeak	Black pudding
Devils on horseback	Cottage pie
Jam roly poly	Brandy snaps
Anglesey eggs	Scotch woodcock

B | CHANGING HABITS

1 Which of the following statements do you think are true?

a The biggest owner of pubs in Britain is a Japanese bank.

b People in Britain are buying 20% less food from supermarkets today than they did ten years ago.

c The British spend about £1.26 billion a year on hamburgers, double what they spend on medicines.

d Over five million kilograms of crisps are eaten in Britain every week.

e There are more Chinese take-aways than there are fish and chip shops in the UK.

f One of the most successful food programmes on TV recently was called 'Two Fat Ladies'. It celebrated some of the richest, heaviest, fattiest foods in British and world cooking.

g In 1997, a frozen food company started selling chocolate-flavoured carrots and pizza-flavoured sweetcorn to encourage children to eat fresh vegetables.

h Just over half the restaurants in Britain are fast-food outlets or takeaways.

i Every person in Britain eats a ready meal from a supermarket at least five times a week.

Check your answers on page 92.

2 The two texts that follow describe recent changes in British eating habits. Read Text A or B. As you read, make a note of any information that suggests a change in the way people live.

Text A

Changes in Average Household Food Consumption 1986-1996

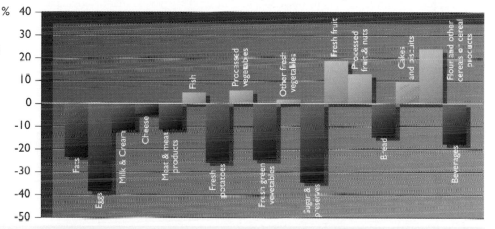

Eating and Drinking Habits

The general level of nutrition remains high. There has been a significant shift in eating patterns over the decade, reflecting greater emphasis on health, frozen and convenience foods. Changes in household consumption of selected foods between 1986 and 1996 are shown in the diagram. Consumption of several items, such as sugar, eggs, fresh potatoes and fresh green vegetables, has declined substantially.

Other changes include:
- a long-term decline in consumption of red meats – beef, lamb and pork – while at the same time consumption of poultry has been rising;
- a rise in fish consumption;
- an increase in purchases of semi-skimmed milks; with skimmed milk now constituting more than half of the total household consumption of liquid milk;
- a decline in the total consumption of cooking and spreading fats, but rapid rises in the consumption of vegetable and salad oils and low-fat spreads;
- a long-term rise in consumption of fresh fruit, such as bananas; and
- a large increase in fruit juice consumption

There has been an increase in the number of meals eaten away from home, for example in restaurants or at work, and a growth in the consumption of food from 'take-away' and 'fast-food' shops.

Alcohol consumption has changed little in recent years. Beer is the most popular drink among male drinkers, whose overall consumption is significantly higher than that of women. A high proportion of beer is drunk in public houses ('pubs'), traditional social centres for many people, and in clubs. Consumption of table wine has grown.

Official Handbook to Britain

35

Text B

Burger Kings March on UK Stomachs

The world's two biggest burger chains, McDonald's and Burger King, are planning big expansions to supply what they believe is the nation's increasing appetite for fast food.

McDonald's intends to open 100 restaurants each year, to add to the 830 it has at present. Its big rival, Burger King, which has 455 restaurants, is to open 55 new outlets this year.

Yesterday Tim Lang, Professor of Food Policy at Thames University, declared himself an opponent. 'I would be congratulating the companies if they were moving into selling fruit and vegetables, but selling more burgers is hardly the sort of advance that the British diet needs,' he said.

Professor Lang believes the American fast food wave has changed our eating habits. We have had fish and chips, Cornish pasties and sandwiches for a long time, but the difference is that the burger chains set up in prime High Street spots to tempt us in.

'We can't say people aren't enjoying it. They are buying it and eating it. But does this represent a wholesome healthy food culture? My honest opinion is no.'

The answer, says Professor Lang, is to get the British back into their kitchens by teaching children to cook.

Children used to learn to cook either at home around the age of 6 to 8 or at school between 12 and 15. Now they miss the second chance and are subjected to the 'burgerisation' attitude of 'why bother to cook when you can nip out and get a burger or a pizza?'

Food analyst Umesh Raichada said of the McDonald's and Burger King plans: 'There is definitely room for this massive expansion. People are eating out much more than they used to. These chains are having to expand now to keep out the competition from pizzas and other ethnic foods. They're hoping to win over stomach share and they want to win it before anyone else does.'

The Guardian

What are the most likely reasons for these changes in your opinion?
Compare your ideas with someone who has read the other text. Show each other what you have read, and explain your conclusions to them.

3

Compare changes in eating habits in your country with those of Britain. Make a list of similarities and differences, and write them up on the board.

C   A TEENAGE DIET

1. A recent issue of the magazine *Shout* examined the diets of three teenage girls and gave a verdict on each one. Read this diary of what one girl ate, then work out (from the three verdicts on the next page) what her name is.

I wouldn't say I was a fussy eater and the only thing I really don't like is fish – I'm always scared I'll swallow a bone! I try to eat a balanced diet and I always have breakfast, lunch and tea which are quite healthy because I have them at home. Sometimes I'm not so good between meals and eat crisps and chocolate, and there's a McDonald's near my house, so it's really easy to go in there and buy a burger! I never used to eat vegetables but I'm starting to eat more of them now. I try to eat fruit fairly often too, but looking at what I've eaten all week, there doesn't seem to be much fruit ...!

SATURDAY
BREAKFAST: Rice Krispies and toast
LUNCH: Chicken soup
MID-AFTERNOON: Cheese and onion crisps, Mars Bar
TEA: Lasagne, chips and garlic bread
IN BETWEEN: 2 Kit Kats
SUPPER: Packet of crisps, toast

SUNDAY
BREAKFAST: Porridge, toast and jam
LUNCH: 2 bread rolls with sausage
MID-AFTERNOON: Stick of rock
TEA: Roast beef, potatoes, cauliflower, roast potatoes, broccoli, sweetcorn, apple pie
IN BETWEEN: Sandwich, Kit Kat
SUPPER: Cornflakes, cheese and onion crisps

MONDAY
BREAKFAST: Porridge and toast
MID-MORNING: Apple
LUNCH: Chicken soup
TEA: Ham salad, pasta and roast potatoes
IN BETWEEN: Tomato flavoured crisps
SUPPER: Crunchy Nut Cornflakes

TUESDAY
BREAKFAST: Porridge
LUNCH: Tomato soup and bread
MID-AFTERNOON: 4 Gingernut biscuits
TEA: Scotch pie, chips and beans
IN BETWEEN: Ice-cream cone, Glacier Mints
SUPPER: Crunchy Nut Cornflakes

WEDNESDAY
BREAKFAST: Porridge
LUNCH: Ham sandwich
MID-AFTERNOON: 2 biscuits
TEA: Spaghetti bolognese and garlic bread, ice-cream and fruit
IN BETWEEN: Wotsits, Monster Munch
SUPPER: Another bowl of Crunchy Nut Cornflakes with ice-cold milk!

SHOUT'S VERDICT

Laura's diet's quite impressive. She has lots of fruit and vegetables and has three meals each day. Apart from the odd sweet Laura's pretty healthy.

SHOUT'S VERDICT

Pamela is pretty healthy – she usually eats three main meals, although she is quite keen on sweets and crisps. If she tried swopping a couple of pieces of fruit for sweets or crisps each day, she could help her diet.

SHOUT'S VERDICT

Lucy's main meals are OK, but her snacks could become a bit more healthy. She should cut down on peanut butter and chocolate spread. If Lucy started to eat breakfast and fruit, her diet would be healthier.

What do you think of the verdict? Add some comments of your own.

2 Make a diary of what you eat in a week. Compare it with others in the class, and with the British girl's. Write a verdict on your diet for readers of *Shout*.

3 ◨◨ Listen to sixth-formers from Edinburgh talking about what they eat. Write notes to compare their diets and yours. Use these headings.

Similarities

....

....

....

....

Differences

....

....

....

....

smilby.

4 The *Shout* article emphasised the importance of breakfast. Is breakfast an important meal for you? What do you eat? Is this typical in your country?

5   Look at the three hotel menus below. Can you label them correctly – Continental, American, British?

Menu 1

Orange juice or
Fresh fruit cocktail

Cereal or Porridge

Bacon, sausage & eggs,
Kedgeree, or Kippers

Toast, rolls
Butter & marmalade

Coffee,
Tea, or
Hot chocolate

Menu 2

Orange juice or
Fresh fruit cocktail

Croissants
Brioches
Butter & jam

Coffee,
Tea, or
Hot chocolate

Menu 3

Orange juice or
Fresh fruit cocktail

Cereal

Ham and eggs
Pancakes & maple syrup

Muffins, bagels
Butter & jam

Coffee,
Tea, or
Hot chocolate

6   Read this passage, and fill in the grid below.

There were few notable changes during the [nineteenth] century, but one striking fact which emerges is the growth in popularity of what has come to be known as the 'typical English breakfast'. While a few of the more leisured people were content with a cup of coffee or tea and rolls or toast, and some of the more old-fashioned remained faithful to the eighteenth-century breakfast of cold meat, cheese and beer, the majority [of wealthy people] adopted the three- or four-course meal of porridge, fish, bacon and eggs, toast and marmalade, which maintained its popularity for a century but which today has been abandoned in favour of a lighter and simpler type of meal.

J. C . Drummond and Anne Wilbraham,
The Englishman's Food

18th century	19th century	Today

D   HOSPITALITY

1 Eating is a social activity, with traditions and codes of behaviour which are taught from earliest childhood. These codes and traditions often vary greatly between cultures.

Think about what you would do if you were invited to a friend's house for dinner in the evening.

What would you wear?

Would you take any presents with you?

How would you behave during the meal?

What would you say afterwards?

2 Read this passage from a book about social customs in Britain.

What details would you change if you were writing about your country?

An invitation to a meal in someone's house usually means a relaxed evening. More often than not men do not wear business suits, while the women wear comfortable rather than fashionable evening clothes. It is a good idea to take some flowers or a box of chocolates for your hostess; some, additionally, bring a bottle of wine. It does not have to be an expensive wine; it is, as we say, the thought that counts. The bottle is hardly ever opened, and quite often serves as a bottle that tonight's host takes as a guest to next week's dinner somewhere else.

In most parts of England (certainly among the middle and upper classes) the hostess expects a short letter of thanks for the evening. Such letters follow a standard formula: you mention the food (how good it was) and the company (how interesting it was) and express the hope that you will meet again soon. The latest fashion is more for a picture postcard (usually from some cultural spot like the National Gallery) with the same kind of note on the back. Traditionalists will expect and write a letter.

Peter Hobday, *The Simple Guide to Customs and Etiquette in England*

3 The variety of cultures within Britain today means that different traditions of hospitality are operating simultaneously, and it's not always easy for people to know how to behave correctly in other people's houses. The novel *Anita and Me* by Meera Syal is about Meena, a Punjabi girl of nine who lives in a mining village in the north of England. She is influenced in conflicting ways by her family and her friends from school, such as Anita.

As you read, try to answer these questions.

1 What surprises or offends Anita about Meena's family?

2 What surprises or offends Meena's family about Anita?

3 What do you find out about different traditions of eating, hospitality, and behaviour at table from this passage?

Anita turned up alone and empty-handed, wearing her new school jumper with a pair of flared jeans. 'Tracey didn't want to come,' was the first thing she said to my parents who stood by the door, as they did for all our visitors, ready to take her coat. 'Oh, that's okay, darling,' said mama, ushering her in and waving at papa to remove one of the place settings from the dining table. I had insisted that we sit at the table, something we never did with Indian guests since we usually ate in shifts. ...

Mama had gone to the trouble of preparing two menus, which was fortunate considering Anita's reaction when the serving dishes of various curries were placed in front of her. 'What's that!' she demanded, as if confronted with a festering sheep's head on a platter. 'Oh that's mattar-paneer,' mama said proudly, always happy to educate the sad English palate. 'A sort of Indian cheese, and these are peas with it, of course ...'

'Cheese and peas?' said Anita faintly. 'Together?'

'Well', mama went on hurriedly. 'This is chicken curry ... You have had chicken before, haven't you?'

'What's that stuff round it?'

'Um, just gravy, you know, tomatoes, onions, garlic ...' Mama was losing confidence now, she trailed off as she picked up Anita's increasing panic.

'Chicken with tomatoes'? What's garlic?'

'Don't you worry!' papa interjected heartily, fearing a culinary cat fight was about to shatter his fragile peace. 'We've also got fishfingers and chips. Is tomato sauce too dangerous for you?'

Anita's relief made her oblivious to his attempt at a joke. She simply picked up her knife and fork and rested her elbows on the table, waiting to be served with something she could recognise. 'I'll have fishfingers, mum! Um, please!' I called out after her. ...

Any romantic idea I had about witty stories over the dinner table disappeared when Anita made a fortress of her arms and chewed stolidly behind it, daring anyone to approach and disturb her concentration or risk losing an eye if they attempted to steal a chip. She looked up only twice, once when my parents began eating, as always, with their fingers, using their chapatti as scoops to ferry the banquet of curries into their mouths.

Anita stopped in mid-chew, looking from her knife and fork to mama and papa's fingers with faint disgust, apparently unaware that all of us had a great view of a lump of half masticated fishfinger sitting on her tongue. It had never occurred to me that this would be a moment of controversy, it had never occurred to me because I had never eaten Indian food in the presence of a white person before. In fact, I only then realised that Anita Rutter was the first non-relative to sit and break bread with us ...

I Think about your schooling so far. What subjects did you take? Tick the boxes.

Subject	Ages 5/6–11	Ages 11–14	Ages 14–16
Mathematics			
Science			
Own language			
Other language 1			
Other language 2			
History			
Geography			
Art			
Music			
PE (physical education)			
RE (religious education)			
IT (information technology)			
Other(s)			

Discuss the following questions.

Which subjects do you think were the most important for you?

Are there subjects which you think are important but which you did not study?

Do you consider that your curriculum had any problems? If you were planning the curriculum, what changes would you like to see, compared to your own programme of study?

What assessments would you have for the subjects? Class tests? National exams? No assessments?

2 Read the text, part of a brochure prepared to inform parents about the National Curriculum in Britain. Compare your own school subjects with those in Britain. What do you think are the advantages or disadvantages of British schooling compared with yours?

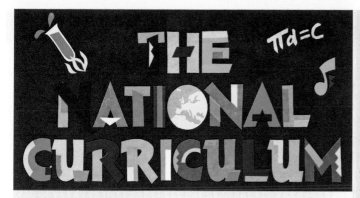

How it works

The National Curriculum subjects are: mathematics, science, English, technology, history, geography, a modern foreign language, art, music and physical education. Religious education is also compulsory.

All pupils will study all subjects.

> **Key stages**
> **Your child's progression through education will have four key stages and assessment will take place at the end of each.**

Generally, each subject has ten levels and your child will progress through one level at a time. The top level is 10 – but not all pupils will reach this level.

An average 16-year-old will attain level 6 or 7

It is unlikely that your child will attain the same level in all areas of study and the National Curriculum has been devised so that pupils can forge ahead in their strong areas of study and get help with their weaker ones.

Here is an example from the programme of study in English.

Between the ages of 14 and 16 pupils will:

- achieve a readable, pleasing writing style
- write effectively about demanding topics
- learn to speak persuasively and clearly, and to use language appropriate to the situation, topic or purpose
- read a wide variety of fiction, poetry and drama, including some pre 20th century works
- interpret, evaluate and compare texts

What do you think of the goals for English? How do they compare with your work in your own language? And with your English course so far?

3 🔲 A group of students on a cultural studies course in England went to visit several schools. They spoke to a teacher at a primary school where the pupils are 5 to 11 years old. Listen and put crosses in the grid in Exercise 1 to show what subjects the children take. Then complete the sentences.

a The children are assessed at ages .... and ....

b The two main subjects that children do in the morning are .... and ....

c The other 'core' subject is ....

d One subject is not on the list above: DT, which stands for ....

e With regard to the curriculum, one of the main problems the school has to face is ....

f The children are at school from 9 in the morning until .... , then from 1 o'clock until .... There are .... school days in the week.

What changes would you make to these sentences so that they were true of your own primary education?

B WHAT ARE SCHOOLS LIKE?

I Read the note about schools in Britain.

> At state schools, parents do not pay fees. At secondary school level, about 5% of children in Britain attend schools which are called 'independent' or 'fee-paying'. Some of the more ancient independent schools are sometimes known as 'public' schools because anyone, regardless of their ethnic background or religion, could send their children there in the nineteenth century, if they could afford it.

The students from Units 5A, Exercise 3 also went to visit an independent secondary school in a suburb of Coventry, Bablake School, where they interviewed the Headmaster. Write down at least three topics which you think were discussed in the interview.

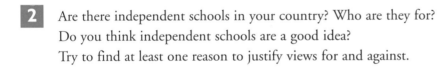 Listen. Are the differences the ones that you expected? Listen again and make notes on

1 how children are selected for the school.
2 exam results at Bablake.
3 differences between Bablake and other independent schools.
4 ethnic groups in the school.

2 Are there independent schools in your country? Who are they for?
Do you think independent schools are a good idea?
Try to find at least one reason to justify views for and against.

3   Listen as one Scottish student sums up his view of his school. What are the important aspects of it for him?
Listen again and, from the context, choose the best meaning for the slang word 'aggro'.

a space   **b** tolerance   **c** violence

Prepare a short description of your school and, if you can, record it for your group or the class.

4 Which of the following issues are talked about by students in your school? Choose the two or three most important ones. Are there others not on the list? Discuss your choices with others.

school clothing	discipline in class
exams	differences in achievement between boys and girls
relations between boys and girls	getting into university
sports	homework
jobs	difficulty with subjects
relations with teachers	

bullying (one or more children being horrible to a particular child, or finding ways to hurt him/her)

5 Here are the headlines and some paragraphs of recent British articles about schools. Match the headlines and the paragraphs.

A

WHAT ABOUT THE CHILDREN?

B

Why uniforms are back in vogue

D

FOOTBALLERS TO THE RESCUE

C

Kids judge the bullies

1

Wearing uniforms to school has long been a peculiarly British idea. It is anathema to the French and Germans, whose thriving state sector has never seen the need for compulsory ties, caps and blazers. But the idea is gaining renewed popularity in state schools, helped along by image-conscious parents. The school uniform in this country has its roots in the public school traditions. Rightly or wrongly, state schools have tended to look to the independent sector for models, and the notion of wearing a uniform has become associated with many people's idea of a good education.

2

More schools are poised to let pupils sit in judgement on classmates accused of bullying. The move is being promoted to curb Britain's classroom violence – the worst in Europe. Education expert Valerie Besag said: 'The secret is to get the kids backing the victim. That way, everyone comes out with credit.'

3

Though much has been said about teacher appraisal, there has been a curious silence about the possible contribution of pupils to the process. In a way it is odd that children, who see more of teachers than anyone else (and from a unique perspective), are not routinely canvassed for their views. This despite the fact that, as is regularly pointed out, it is children who are the real 'consumers' of education.

4

[One inner-city school in Bristol tried a scheme of special 'achievement' classes to help deprived children learn to read.]
The results have been very satisfying, but one group is still progressing much faster than the other. And that is the girls. The Achievement lessons were closely graded into 12 different groups according to ability. And the girls outnumbered the boys by a ratio of two to one in the top groups. 'It is still often seen as unmacho for boys to be keen on schoolwork ... Partly, this is because many boys have so few male academic role models. ... The National Curriculum is heavily weighted in favour of coursework at which girls traditionally excel. Maybe it is time to think about restructuring a more boy-friendly curriculum.'
[One solution was inviting footballers to talk to the boys.]

6 Which of the issues in Exercise 4 are featured in these articles?
Which fact or opinion did you find most interesting in the articles?

7 Match each sentence with a speech bubble that has a similar meaning.

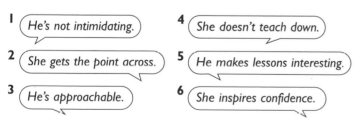

1 (He's not intimidating.)
2 (She gets the point across.)
3 (He's approachable.)
4 (She doesn't teach down.)
5 (He makes lessons interesting.)
6 (She inspires confidence.)

a The teacher isn't boring.
b It's easy to talk to the teacher.
c We trust the teacher.
d The teacher doesn't frighten us.
e The teacher treats us with respect.
f The teacher explains things simply.

What do you think are the most important qualities in a teacher?
List at least three and compare with others.

8 Listen to the answers given by five students from Bristol. Tick any of the words in Exercise 7 that are mentioned by the students. Are their views close to your own?

C WHAT ARE CLASSES LIKE?

1 Here is an extract from a contemporary British play, which begins inside a classroom in East London. Work in groups. Choose one of the tasks.

a Prepare a dramatic reading of the extract from the play. Present it to the class.

b Write a scene for the play, to show the next time Joe meets his class in the afternoon and has a chat with them.

c Prepare a dramatised version of a typical day in your school. Present it to the class.

Babies by Jonathan Harvey

Scene One

*9CY's tutor base, in a modern south east London comprehensive school. There is a teacher's desk and the front row of four students' desks and chairs. At these desks sit **Kelly**, **Simone**, **David** and **Richard**. Their backs are to the audience. Supposedly the rest of the class are where the audience are, so when a character talks or looks to the audience, they are in fact addressing another classmate.*

*On the teacher's desk sits **Joe Casey**, taking the register. He is the form tutor.*

*The kids are dressed in modern school uniform: navy blue trousers, sweatshirt and trainers. They each have a 'Head' bag, in different colours, except **Kelly**, who has a plastic bag. **David** also has an oboe case. They are all about thirteen/fourteen.*

***Joe Casey** wears jeans and a leather jacket, he is twenty-four. Whereas the kids all speak in broad south east London accents, **Joe** speaks with a broad Liverpool twang.*

*As **Joe** takes the register there are various replies of 'here', 'yeah', and 'yo Sir' from the class. **Simone** swings round in her chair and chats with her mate **Angel**, behind her.*

JOE	Kelly	*At the same time.*		SIMONE	What? Oh here Sir.
	Lee			JOE	Face the front Simone.
	Donna	SIMONE (*whisper*) Angel! Angel!		SIMONE (*tuts*)	Tell me in science. (*Turning*). Yeah Sir.
	Kellie	Did you see him? ...		JOE	Kaylee
	Lee	What d'he say?			Justin
	Simon	Did you tell him? Was he gutted?			Leah
					Gurjit
	Angel	Are you ...?			Vicki
	Lee-Anne	Sit on our bench in science. I			Robert
	Terry	wanna know everything.			Wayne
		Yeah ...			and Tammy. Oh yeah. (*Closes register.*) Actually, eyes front 9CY.
	Osman	Oh no he didn't! ...			You too, Balvinder. Right, a word,
	David	Have you seen Lee-Anne			please. (*Burps.*) Pardon me.
	Richard	Benner's culottes? ...		SIMONE	Better out than in.
	Kelly-Ann	I know!		JOE	Thanks Simone. Now, I want yous
	Sukhvinder	Mark One or what?			all to cast your minds back, if you
	Balvinder	(*Laughs.*)			will, to the end of last term. Yeah?
	Simone. Simone? Who give you that black eye?				

Remember that day I sent Tammy on the errand with the staple gun? And I told you all her dad was really ill with cancer? Mm? Well you've probably noticed, but Tammy's not been in school this week.

KELLY (*to Simone*) Her dad's died.

SIMONE Has he?

JOE Well most of you probably know by now, but Tammy's dad died at the weekend.

KELLY Sir. Simone's crying.

JOE Okay.

KELLY (*to Simone*) Do it louder. (*Simone's crying gets louder.*)

JOE Now when Tammy comes back to school, how d'you think we should all behave? Bearing in mind that her dad's just died.

DAVID Sir, be dead nice and that.

RICHARD Shut up Simone!

JOE Yeah. Be supportive to her. That's a really important word, yeah? Support. I mean just imagine how you'd feel if your dad had just died, or your mum ... or your guardian ... I know I'd be dead sad. So (*Beat.*) No, Balvinder, you wouldn't be over the moon. Balvinder! (*Class giggles.*) Now look here, if I catch any of yous taking the mickey, I'll send you straight to Miss Sterry and we'll see what she's got to say shall we?

RICHARD She's a lesbian!

JOE Thank you Richard.

KELLY Is she Sir?

RICHARD She's a moany old cow!

JOE Er excuse me! We don't and I repeat *don't* talk like that about members of staff in this room, do we?

RICHARD *tuts.*

JOE Do we?

RICHARD No Sir.

JOE Thank you. Sexuality is a private and personal thing. Okay? Now a word about your homeworks please, that was the worksheet: 'Cinderella Fights Back'.

KELLY Sir can I take Simone to the toilet?

JOE Er ...

KELLY Her mascara's run.

JOE Give us your diary.

Simone goes in her bag for her school diary. She takes out twenty Bensons and a lighter and slips them in her pocket. She then finds her diary. Kelly has jumped out of her seat. She links arms with Joe.

KELLY Ah cheers Sir. In'e a blinding teacher, eh?

JOE (*releasing her arm*) What's the rule on physical contact?

* * *

He opens Simone's diary. Just then seven warning pips sound, heralding the end of registration. Sounds of pandemonium breaking out.

JOE Oh why are there never enough minutes in the day? Okay, pack your things up and get off to science. I'll have that chat this afternoon.

2 What do you think of Joe as a teacher?

D | WHAT HAPPENS AFTER SECONDARY SCHOOL?

1 The school leaving age in Britain is 16. Study the flow chart showing the possibilities for young people in Britain from age 16.

Would a chart for your country show many differences from this one? What are the main differences?

Educational possibilities for Young People in Britain from Age 16.

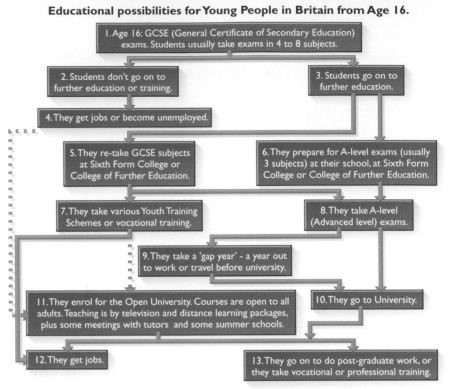

1. Age 16: GCSE (General Certificate of Secondary Education) exams. Students usually take exams in 4 to 8 subjects.

2. Students don't go on to further education or training.

3. Students go on to further education.

4. They get jobs or become unemployed.

5. They re-take GCSE subjects at Sixth Form College or College of Further Education.

6. They prepare for A-level exams (usually 3 subjects) at their school, at Sixth Form College or College of Further Education.

7. They take various Youth Training Schemes or vocational training.

8. They take A-level (Advanced level) exams.

9. They take a 'gap year' - a year out to work or travel before university.

11. They enrol for the Open University. Courses are open to all adults. Teaching is by television and distance learning packages, plus some meetings with tutors and some summer schools.

10. They go to University.

12. They get jobs.

13. They go on to do post-graduate work, or they take vocational or professional training.

OPTION

Create a poster, showing the possibilities for young people in your country.

2 Study the four statements about school leavers in the 1990s. Then look at the graph. The title of Column 4 is: NO PLANS. Match each of the columns 1, 2 and 3 with one of these titles:

Youth Training   Employment   Education

a More young people are now leaving school without any plans for their future.

b In the 1990s, only 15% of young people went straight into work, compared with over 30% in the Eighties.

c There has been a decline in numbers joining youth training schemes.

d Record numbers of 16-year-olds are staying in education, as youth unemployment rates rise. Well over 60% are now in education. This shows that Britain is catching up with Europe, Japan and America, where 90% of 16-year-olds continue schooling.

A comparison between the Eighties and the Nineties

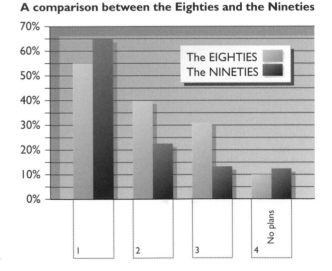

The EIGHTIES
The NINETIES

What about your country? Do you know the figures for students staying on in education after 16?

3 In England, university entrance is based on the results of the A-level exams, but there are a number of steps which many pupils go through in the two years before university. Here are some of the main ones. How many of them are also necessary in your country?

a Visit the careers office at school.

b Discuss their choice of universities with their teacher or headteacher.

c Send off for prospectuses from various universities (brochures which describe the university and its courses).

d Visit the universities they are interested in (go to 'open days').

e Apply to the universities by filling in a form listing five choices.

f Take school exams: the results are used to predict A-level results, and are recorded on university applications.

4 Read the following extract, published in a newspaper, from the diary of a 'lower-sixth' student (a student in the first of her two years of study leading up to the A-level exams). In what order did she take the steps above?

February

Mum still nagging me to write to universities, but I haven't quite got round to it.

March

Have finally sent off for some prospectuses – and actually found them quite interesting. Have spent several lunchtimes in the careers room.

May

Plodding on with four A-levels as well as all other activities. Went to an open day at Bristol and am thinking much more seriously about university.

June

The month lower-sixths dread: time for the exams on which A-level predictions for university are based. I survive and am pleased with my marks. Maybe they will make my parents realise that I do have the balance between work and other activities right.

July

Been to more open days, and my attention has been focused a lot more on university. I have to sort out my application immediately after the summer holidays. Had an interview with the headmistress to discuss Oxford. The good news is that she says I could hardly be a stronger candidate. The bad news is, I really don't know whether I want to go to Oxford after all.

September

This is it, the upper-sixth. I've finally made a decision about Oxford – I really don't want to go there. I do want to go to Exeter. I've given up my Saturday job, and I've made a resolution to get down to some serious study. A-levels are closer than we think.

5 Is applying for university easy or stressful in your country? How did it seem to be for the writer of the diary?

OPTION

Write some entries for your diary on one of these.

Exam week at school or college

Making career plans

A typical week at school or university.

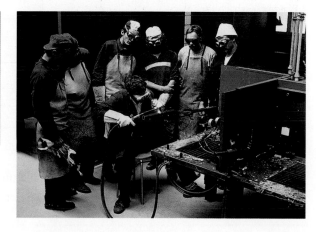

A   WHAT DO YOU DO IN YOUR FREE TIME?

1   What do you do in your free time?
Make a list on the board of your leisure
activities – list all those in which you
participate at least once a week.

2   Here are the results of a recent survey about the most popular leisure activities in Britain.
Try to guess whether the percentages for 16- to 24-year-olds is higher (+) or lower (-)
than for the population as a whole.

What people do – % participation – at least once a week

Activity	% of all people	% of 16- to 24-year-olds + or – ?
Watching TV	96	
Reading newspapers	80	
Listening to the radio	73	
Reading books	60	
Listening to CDs/tapes/records	58	
Watching videos (recorded programmes)	47	
Playing with children	47	
Gardening	42	
Playing with pets	41	
Reading magazines	40	
Cooking for pleasure	37	
Visiting a pub in the evening	36	
Watching other videos	30	

You can look up the percentages for young people on page 93.
How similar is your own list to the most popular activities in the survey?

3 🔲 Listen to three English students at a boarding school answering the question:
'What do you do in your leisure time?'
Write 1, 2 or 3 to show which students

a feel that there isn't much spare time in the day. ◯
b have a lot of work to do outside class. ◯
c enjoy shopping as a leisure time activity. ◯
d work for the school's Internet website. ◯
e are studying a foreign language. ◯
f like to visit the nearby city. ◯
g are musical. ◯
h enjoy socializing in their spare time. ◯
i have some responsibility for catering. ◯
   (catering = making food arrangements)
j would like to do more sport. ◯

4 🔲 Work with a partner.
Listen to Scottish students
answering the question:
'What do you do on a
typical Saturday evening?'

PARTNER A	PARTNER B
Make notes about students 1 and 3.	Make notes about students 2 and 4.

5 Now make a second list on the board, this time of the most popular leisure activities for
English and Scottish students. Are there significant differences between them and your own?

What did you find most interesting or surprising about the survey – or about the answers
given by the English and Scottish students?

6 Look again at the table in Exercise 2. Can you guess the average number
of hours each British household spends watching TV every week?
a 7   b 21   c 28   d 42

You can find the answer on page 92.

7 What do you think of watching TV as a leisure activity? Write down as many advantages and
disadvantages as you can think of.

8 Read this song from *Charlie and The Chocolate Factory* by Roald Dahl.

The most important thing we've learned,
So far as children are concerned,
Is never, NEVER, NEVER let
Them near your television set –
Or better still, just don't install
The idiotic thing at all.
In almost every house we've been,
We've watched them gaping at the screen.
They loll and slop and lounge about,
And stare until their eyes pop out.
(Last week in someone's place we saw
A dozen eyeballs on the floor.)
They sit and stare and stare and sit
Until they're hypnotized by it.
Until they're absolutely drunk
With all that shocking ghastly junk.
Oh yes, we know it keeps them still,
They don't climb out the window sill,
They never fight or kick or punch,
They leave you free to cook the lunch
And wash the dishes in the sink –
But did you ever stop to think,
To wonder just exactly what
This does to your beloved tot?
IT ROTS THE SENSES IN THE HEAD!
IT KILLS IMAGINATION DEAD!
IT CLOGS AND CLUTTERS UP THE MIND!
IT MAKES A CHILD SO DULL AND BLIND
HE CAN NO LONGER UNDERSTAND
A FANTASY, A FAIRYLAND!
HIS BRAIN BECOMES AS SOFT AS CHEESE!
HIS POWERS OF THINKING RUST AND FREEZE!
HE CANNOT THINK – HE ONLY SEES!

'All right!' you'll cry. 'All right!' you'll say,
'But if we take the set away,
What shall we do to entertain
Our darling children! Please explain!'
We'll answer this by asking you,
'What used the darling ones to do?
How *used* they keep themselves contented
Before this monster was invented?'
Have you forgotten? Don't you know?
We'll say it very loud and slow:
THEY … USED … TO … READ! They'd READ and READ,
AND READ and READ, and then proceed
TO READ some more. Great Scott! Gadzooks!
One half their lives was reading books!
The nursery shelves held books galore!
Books cluttered up the nursery floor!
And in the bedroom, by the bed,
More books were waiting to be read!
Such wondrous, fine, fantastic tales
Of dragons, gypsies, queens, and whales
And treasure isles, and distant shores
Where smugglers rowed with muffled oars,
And pirates wearing purple pants,
And sailing ships and elephants,
And cannibals crouching round the pot,
Stirring away at something hot.
(It smells so good, what can it be?
Good gracious, it's Penelope.)

* * *

So please, oh *please*, we beg, we pray,
Go throw your TV set away,
And in its place you can install
A lovely bookshelf on the wall.

Do you agree with the views in this song? Or do you think they are exaggerated?
Do you think they are more relevant to children than to adults?

9 Choose one of the following.

a Write a poem in the same style, expressing your own views about television.
b Write a letter to a child you know, giving some advice about what to do in their free time.

B TELEVISION

1 Here are descriptions of different kinds of television programmes. Find the right name for each one.

a An exciting story, often involving criminals and the police, which builds up an atmosphere of fear or suspense

b A programme which offers a description and analysis of political, social or historical events

c A fictional story about a group of people, usually in a specific social setting, broadcast at regular times throughout the week and sometimes lasting for years

d A factual programme showing the lives of animals or insects

e A summary of the events of the day in the country and throughout the world, usually with weather forecasts

f A programme that shows or discusses a game, match or other sports event

g A programme in which a well-known interviewer talks to famous guests

h A question-and-answer competition between teams

i A fictional story set in the past – often adapted from a famous novel

j A series of funny stories about the same group of characters.

> **1** A soap (soap opera) **2** The news and weather **3** A thriller **4** A historical drama **5** A quiz show
>
> **6** A comedy series **7** A wildlife programme **8** A chat show **9** A sports programme **10** A documentary

What kind of television programme do you like best? Would you add any categories to the ones above?

2 Imagine that you wish to propose either a drama series or a documentary for your own country.
Decide about setting, themes, story, style and characters (or people to interview).
Consider all the ideas in the class. Which would you most like to see on TV?

3 What do you think it is like to plan and make a television programme? Is it likely to be friendly and relaxed, or stressful?
Read the two extracts on page 54. Then answer these questions.

1 What kind of television programme is being made in each case?

2 What sort of people are Lord Mellow and Richard Finch?

3 What do you think it would be like to work with them?

Extract A
Cuts, by Malcom Bradbury

Lord Mellow is the chief executive of a TV company. In this extract, he calls a meeting of his production team.

'Right,' said Lord Mellow, coming in, sitting down heavily at his big white desk, and looking round the group. 'Who's going to jump out of the window first? I want someone to jump out of that window and stain the pavement. I don't care who, but I want it right away.'

'Evidently some error has occurred,' said Lord Lenticule, the oldest board member. 'I say no more than that.'

'I'll say an error has occurred,' said Lord Mellow. 'I spent half a million getting that script developed.'

'Lord Mellow,' said Jocelyn Pride, 'we did actually discuss it in detail with you.'

'You thought it had everything,' said Cynthia Hyde-Lemon, in her big yellow jumpsuit.

'Great country houses, royals, political conflict, the Irish question, lots of Empire,' said Jocelyn Pride. 'Beautiful locations, India, the Crimea …' said a man in a bow-tie: the head of Technical Staff.

'Ireland, the Balkans,' added Jocelyn Pride.

'Liverpool for grim actuality,' put in Cynthia Hyde-Lemon …

'I never liked it,' said Lord Mellow. 'I never wanted it. Now I want that script shredded. I want it pulped. I want the waste paper sold abroad.' …

'Yesterday you said you liked the script,' said Cynthia.

'I was lying, to save you pain,' said Lord Mellow.

'So what do you want, Lord Mellow?' asked Cynthia.

'What I want is something international and of this moment,' he said. 'With love and joy in it, along with a little pain. So let's all start thinking, really thinking, all over again.'

There was a silence.

Extract B
Bridget Jones's Diary, by Helen Fielding

This novel is written in the form of a diary. In the extract, Bridget, a young reporter, has just joined a company that makes programmes for television, and she is rather nervous and anxious to prove to her boss, Richard Finch, that she can do the job.

Tuesday 26 September

The really exciting news is that I am going to be given a try-out in front of the camera.

Richard Finch got this idea into his head at the end of last week that he wanted to do a Live Action Special with reporters attached to emergency services all over the capital. He didn't have much luck to start with. In fact people were going round the office saying he had been turned down by every Accident and Emergency Unit, Police and Ambulance Force in the Home Counties. But this morning when I arrived he grabbed me by the shoulders yelling 'Bridget! We're on! Fire. I want you on camera. I'm thinking mini-skirt. I'm thinking fireman's helmet. I'm thinking pointing the hose.'

Anyway, it is all happening tomorrow and I have to report to Lewisham fire station at 11 o'clock. I'm going to ring round everybody tonight and tell them to watch. Cannot wait to tell Mum.

Wednesday 27 September

9pm Have never been so humiliated in my life. Spent all day rehearsing and getting everything organized. The idea was that when they cut to Lewisham I was going to slide down the pole into shot and start interviewing a fireman. At five o'clock as we went on air I was perched at the top of the pole ready to slide down on my cue. Then suddenly in my earpiece I heard Richard shouting 'Go, go, go, go, go!' so I let go of the pole and started to slide. Then he continued 'Go, go, go Newcastle! Bridget, stand by in Lewisham. Coming to you in thirty seconds.'

I thought about dropping to the bottom of the pole and rushing back up the stairs but I was only a few feet down so I started to pull myself up instead. Then suddenly there was a great bellow in my ear.

'Bridget! We're on you. What are you doing? You're meant to be sliding down the pole, not climbing up it. Go, go, go.'

Hysterically I grinned at the camera and dropped myself down, landing, as scheduled, by the feet of the fireman I was supposed to interview.

'Lewisham, we're out of time. Wind it up, wind it up, Bridget' yelled Richard in my ear.

'And now back to the studio,' I said, and that was it.

Thursday 28 September

11 am Am in disgrace and am laughing stock. 'And now back to the studio,' seems to have turned into a new catchphrase in the office. Any time anyone gets asked a question they don't know the answer to they go, 'Errrr … and now back to the studio', and burst out laughing.

C CINEMA

1 How many of these films and famous British actors do you recognise? Match the names and the pictures.

Films	Shirley Valentine Gandhi The Pink Panther The Full Monty From Russia With Love
	Sense and Sensibility

Actors	Alec Guinness Kate Winslet Elizabeth Taylor Kenneth Branagh Michael Caine
	Emma Thompson Helena Bonham Carter Anthony Hopkins

Share your results and discuss them. How many of the films have you seen? Are there others you remember?

2 How often do you go to the cinema? What kind of films do you like to see? Compare ideas in your class.

3 🔊 Listening puzzle. Seven students answered the question: 'How often do you go to the cinema?' Listen and fill in as many details as you can. Some squares in the grid will remain blank. Then read the clues and work out the name of each of the students.

Number	How often?	What kind of film?	Time problem?	Money problem?	Name?
1					
2					
3					
4					
5					
6					
7					

Clues

1 The cost of cinema-going is a problem for Kay and Sheena, but not for Bill.
2 Simon and David both say they go to the cinema quite often.
3 Sheena and Bill both say they go to the cinema quite regularly.
4 Alex and Paul say they don't go to the cinema very much, but actually Paul goes about as often as Simon.
5 Finding time to go to the cinema is a problem for Simon and Kay.
6 David and Sheena like comedies, but David likes action films as well.

4 How much do you know about the cinema industry in your country? Can you answer these questions?

a How many films are made in your country on average every year?
b Is the number of films being made going up?
c What successful films have been made in recent years?
d Does the government fund the film industry?

You'll find the answers for Britain on page 93.

5 Is there a film which you would choose to show what your country is like?
Write a short description of it.

6 🔊 Listen to this interview with the film director Tim Fywell and answer the questions.

a How did he become a film director? Choose the right answer.
   His father was in the film business.
   He was originally an actor.
   He started by making commercials.
   He did a directing course with the BBC.
   A friend asked him to direct a script.
b What is his favourite film?
c What does he like about his job?
d What does he dislike about his job?
e What are the main differences in his experience between film-making in Britain and the USA?
f What is his reaction to the scenes from *Cuts* and *Bridget Jones's Diary*?

D THEATRE

I You are organising a school trip to Britain for August next year. You are keen to go to the theatre during your stay.

GROUP A	GROUP B	GROUP C
Read Text A about theatres in London. **Persuade the rest of the class that London is the place for a thrilling theatrical weekend.**	**Read Text B about theatres in Stratford-upon-Avon.** **Plan a weekend there and persuade the rest of the class to come with you.**	**Read Text C about the Edinburgh Festival Fringe, and convince the class that they should go there to see the most exciting theatre in Britain.**

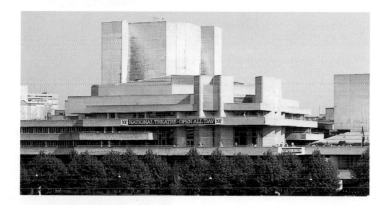

Text A

LONDON has enjoyed a reputation for quality theatre since the time of Shakespeare, and despite the increasing prevalence of fail-safe blockbuster musicals the city still provides a platform for innovation. From the Victorian splendour of the major West End theatres to the stark modernism of the South Bank Centre, London has a plethora of major stages, while the more experimental fringe circuit makes use of a vast array of buildings all over the city.

The comedy scene is just as vibrant – mostly in clubs and pubs, although those comedians who have made the transition to television often crop up with shows in major theatres. The comedy and cabaret circuit continues to disgorge a stream of fast-thinking young wits, and some cabaret-type venues also command a devoted following for their poetry readings.

In fact few cities in the world can match the variety of the London scene. The government-subsidized Royal Shakespeare Company and the National Theatre ensure that the masterpieces of the mainstream tradition remain in circulation, often in productions of startling originality. Many of the West End's commercial theatres have been hijacked by long-running musicals or similarly unchallenging shows, but others offer more intriguing productions. London's fringe theatres, whether they be cosy pub venues or converted warehouses, offer a good spread of classic and contemporary work, while some of the most exciting work is mounted by various small theatre companies that have no permanent base.

fail-safe blockbuster musicals: popular musical shows that are always profitable

fringe circuit: small, informal places around the capital, where plays are put on

comedy and cabaret circuit: local pubs and cafés where comedians perform

a venue: the place where a play is put on

the mainstream tradition: the best known plays in literature

London, The Rough Guide

Text B

STRATFORD-UPON-AVON is an unremarkable market town but for one little detail: in 1564, the wife of a local merchant, John Shakespeare, gave birth to William Shakespeare, probably the greatest writer ever to use the English language ...

There was no theatre in Stratford in Shakespeare's day – it was not until 1769 that Stratford organized any event in honour of him, and that was a festival put together by London-based actor-manager David Garrick, which featured no dramatic performances at all. From then on, the idea of building a permanent home in which to perform Shakespeare's works gained momentum, and the feasibility of building a theatre in backwater Stratford grew immensely with the advent of better roads and the railways. The first memorial Theatre opened in 1879, on land donated by local beer magnate Charles Flower, who also funded the project.

After a fire in 1926 the competition held for a replacement was won by the only woman applicant, Elisabeth Scott. Her theatre, overlooking a beautiful scene of lush meadows and willow trees on the northern banks of the Avon, is today the Main House, presenting a constant diet of Shakespeare's works. At the back, the burnt-out original theatre has been converted into a replica 'in-the-round' Elizabethan stage – named The Swan, it's used for works by Shakespeare's contemporaries, classics from all eras, and one annual piece by the man himself. A third auditorium, The Other Place, in nearby Southern Lane, showcases modern and experimental pieces.

As the Royal Shakespeare Company works on a repertory system, you could stay in Stratford for a few days and see four or five different plays. During the day you can inspect the Royal Shakespeare Company's trove of theatrical memorabilia at the RSC Collection, or go on a backstage tour.

In Stratford you can also visit the Shakespeare Centre and Birthplace Museum; Holy Trinity Church, which contains Shakespeare's tomb; Hall's Croft, the former home of Shakespeare's elder daughter, Susanna, and her doctor husband, John Hall – now a fascinating museum of Elizabethan medicine; the beautiful gardens and foundations of New Place (Shakespeare's last residence, demolished in 1759); Anne Hathaway's Cottage, the home of the woman who in 1582 became Shakespeare's wife; Mary Arden's House, an Elizabethan country farm, formerly the home of Shakespeare's mother; and the Shakespeare Countryside Museum.

Britain, The Rough Guide

gained momentum: grew in strength

backwater: a sleepy little place where nothing much happens

the advent of: the coming of

a beer magnate: a person who has become very rich by making beer

to showcase: to select and publicize

trove of theatrical memorabilia: precious souvenirs of past productions

Text C

THE EDINBURGH FESTIVAL, now the largest arts festival in the world, first took place in August 1947. Driven by a desire for reconciliation and escape from postwar austerity, the Austrian conductor, Rudolf Bing, brought together a host of distinguished musicians from the war-ravaged countries of central Europe. The symbolic centrepiece of his vision was the emotional reunion of Bruno Walter, a Jewish refugee from Nazi tyranny, and the Vienna Philharmonic Orchestra. At the same time, eight theatrical groups, both Scottish and English, turned up in Edinburgh, uninvited, performing in an unlikely variety of local venues, thus establishing the Fringe. Today the festival attracts a million people to the city over three weeks (the last three in August, or the last fortnight and the first week in September) and encompasses several separate festivals, each offering a wide variety of artists and events – everything is on show, from the highbrow to the controversial ...

For many years, the official Edinburgh International Festival was dominated by opera. Although, in the 1980s, efforts were made to involve locals and provide a broader cultural mix of international theatre, dance and classical music, the official festival is still very much a high-brow event ...

The Festival Fringe began to really take off in the 1970s. Set up in 1951, the Fringe Society has grown from a small group to today's large-scale operation serving an annual influx of more than five hundred acts – national theatre groups to student troupes – using around two hundred venues. In spite of this expansion, the Fringe has remained loyal to the original open door policy and there is still no vetting of performers. This means that the shows range from the inspired to the truly diabolical and ensures a highly competitive atmosphere, in which one bad review in a prominent publication means box-office disaster. Many unknowns rely on self-publicity, taking to the streets to perform highlights from their show, or pressing leaflets into the hands of every passer-by. Performances go on round the clock: if so inclined, you could sit through twenty shows in a day.

There is a also a Film Festival, a Jazz Festival, and a Book Festival.

Britain, The Rough Guide

postwar austerity: hard times after the second world war

a symbolic centrepiece: the main and most significant part

a venue: the place where a play is put on

highbrow: considered part of high, elite culture

the Fringe: plays, often experimental in nature, put on in smaller places

to take off: to be successful

open door policy: a policy which allows all plays to be put on, without any 'vetting' or selection by a committee

a box-office disaster: a very unprofitable production, one that loses money

2 Look at this picture, taken recently at the Edinburgh Festival.

What kind of play do you think is being performed here? Write a few lines of the play you imagine – either a monologue by one of the people or a dialogue between them.

THE SMALLEST THEATRE IN THE WORLD

NEWSPAPERS, MAGAZINES, BOOKS

A   READING HABITS

1 Here are the covers of some popular British magazines.

Which ones would you be interested in? Why?

2 What newspapers, magazines and books do you read? Fill in this questionnaire.

QUESTIONNAIRE

First name: ....   Age: ....   Home town: ....

1 What magazines or comics do you read? ....

What do you like about them? ....

....

2 What books have you had to read in the last year? ....

What books have you chosen to read in the last year? ....

Which ones have you liked? Write a few lines about one or two that you've particularly enjoyed. ....

....

3 Do you read a newspaper? Which one(s)? ....

What part of the newspaper do you like best? ....

3 Here are some answers to Question 1 from British students.

> What similarities are there between their answers and yours?
>
> What are the differences?
>
> Does anything surprise you in the British students' answers?

Choose a student whose answers interest you. Imagine meeting him/her.
What sort of person do you think he/she might be?

---

1 First name: Susie   Age: 16   Home town: Oxford

What magazines or comics do you read? The Big Issue, Q, Vox, BBC clothes show, Elle, Vogue, The Face, i-D, Select

What do you like about them? They keep you up to date on good (cheap sometimes) clothes, and music trends. Also tell you about (music) clubs and festivals.

---

1 First name: Sophie   Age: 16   Home town: Belfast

What magazines or comics do you read? Sugar, Bliss, More, 19, Mizz, Just 17

What do you like about them? Full of stories, problems, horoscopes

---

1 First name: Louise   Age: 18   Home town: Banbridge

What magazines or comics do you read? Cosmopolitan, The Clothes Show magazine, Empire

What do you like about them? They have up to date issues – e.g. animal testing. Also fashion & music & interviews with celebrities, politicians, etc. Empire has all up to date films, how they were made, etc.

---

1 First name: Ariel   Age: 16   Home town: London

What magazines or comics do you read? TNT Magazine

What do you like about them? It's free. You don't have to pay for it. It reminds me, and informs me, of my true home – Australia (that is serious!)

B MAGAZINES

1 You are going to read an article about a visit by a British pop group to Sarajevo in the summer of 1996. (British artists and entertainers often help to raise money for victims of AIDS, famine, war, etc.) Before you read, make some notes about the subject.

> What do you expect the article to tell you?
> What would you like to know?

Compare your notes with a partner.

2 Check your vocabulary by matching the words on the left with the definitions on the right.

chart busters	concert
state-of-the-art	close friends
donated	restricted
sound system (or PA)	main singer of a group
rationed	containing the latest technology
gig	place where concerts are held
get in people's way	less famous band who play first at a concert
venue	time when everyone must be off the streets
support group	given as a present
lead singer	loudspeakers, microphones and amplifiers
mates	people in charge of a recording
producers	successful pop stars
curfew	make life difficult for others

Now read the article.

A seriously Dodgy road trip

The Serious Road Trip helped Dodgy deliver more than just a sound system to Bosnia. Fiona Macdonald-Smith went with them.

When British chart busters Dodgy decide to play Sarajevo, a party of journalists goes with them to record the occasion – by plane. For The Big Issue the journey is less luxurious – in the lorry with the sound system.

After two hours loading cargo we are ready to go by 4.30am. Tim tells me not to bother with seat belts because, in the event of a crash, 'It's safer going through the windscreen than being hit from behind by several tonnes of equipment'. On this encouraging note, we set off on a three-day drive.

Our cargo is no ordinary sound system. It is a state-of-the-art eight-kilowatt Turbosound PA bought with the money donated to The Serious Road Trip, which has delivered more than 3,000 tonnes of aid to the former

Yugoslavia. Now that the Sarajevans are trying to return to normal life, music and the arts are an important part of the healing process. Yet in a city where water and electricity are rationed to a few hours each day, finding the necessary equipment is a complicated process.

There are only two sound systems in Sarajevo, and according to one local aid worker, 'both of them belong to the local mafia and they're pretty bad anyway'. So it's no small gift.

Dodgy – or Andy, Nigel and Matthew – are doing the Bosnian gig for free and are feeling slightly nervous. Not just because it's a recent war zone, but because, as Matthew puts it, 'we don't want to get in people's way, have them saying "what are you doing here? What do you think you can do with that guitar?"'

By the time we arrive, it's only a few hours before the gig, but the band's instruments are still at the Slovenian border, because they didn't have the necessary documentation. The venue, the cellar-like Kik club, is in a Sarajevo suburb relatively free of bombed-out buildings. The concert is indoors rather than the planned outdoor venue, because Dodgy couldn't raise the money to pay for the insurance.

But when the band eventually plays to the crowded club (with instruments borrowed from local support group Sikter), no one really cares. 'This is a great day in Dodgy's history,' shouts lead singer Nigel, as a group of young fans dance enthusiastically at the front.

Tomorrow Dodgy will be going to Zagreb, then on to Rimini. 'Tour Europe, tour Japan, tour some more, try and write songs, try and buy some Christmas presents,' says Matthew, the band's drummer, mourning his lost personal life. 'One thing I don't like is when you get old mates that you haven't seen for five years saying, "you don't call me any more Mr Pop Star", and I feel like saying, "well you don't call me anymore, Mr Postman". If I haven't called them it's because I've been busy.'

'But I shouldn't complain. It's what we always wanted,' he adds hastily.

The PA system will stay at the university, as part of the Kuk Project – a community music project run jointly by The Serious Road Trip and the University of Sarajevo. It aims to get people of all ages involved in music, from hearing bands playing to taking music therapy into the local psychiatric hospital. The new term in September will provide training for technicians and producers. 'If bands can get here now, they can play – we've got everything we need to make a concert,' says The Serious Road Trip's Simon Clinn, who is based at the project.

Dodgy aren't the first band to play Sarajevo – China Drum, Joan Baez and Bruce Dickinson (ex-Iron Maiden) have all made appearances. But record labels and particularly their insurers are still cautious about playing in Bosnia. The fact that the new equipment is in place might make them realise it is not impossible. Simon would like to see the day when Sarajevo is just part of the European music circuit – when it's not seen as something unique to play there. Only then can music be part of the healing process for everyone, not just the students at the university, or the children at the psychiatric hospital. 'If we're talking about special needs, virtually everyone in Sarajevo has a special need at the moment,' he says.

For now, the several hundred teenagers spilling out onto the lit pavement outside the club look like any other group of young people in a European city enjoying themselves on a Saturday night. But here the music only lasts until the 11pm curfew, and then the light and laughter is swallowed up by the dark.

The Big Issue

3 Did the article tell you what you wanted to know?
What did you think of it generally?

4 Now read the article again and answer these questions.

a Of the twelve paragraphs, which ones tell the story of what actually happened on the trip?

b What do the other paragraphs tell you about?

c Look at the first paragraph. What do you think is the point of contrasting journalists who travel by plane and the writer who goes in the lorry?

d Look at the last paragraph. Do you think this is an effective end? What does it suggest to you?

e Find some indications in the article that the trip might be
 – dangerous
 – badly organised in some ways
 – well organised in some ways

f 'Music and the arts are an important part of the healing process'. Does the article explain this idea? Do you agree?

C   NEWSPAPERS

1   Look back to the questionnaire on page 60. Compare your answers to Question 3 with other students. Do most people in the class read newspapers? Do they read the same or different ones? Which parts of the newspaper are most popular?

2   Look at these statements about newspapers in Britain. Adapt them so they are true of your country.

There are ten national newspapers.

The national newspapers are of three kinds: 'quality', 'middle market' and 'popular'.

There are special Sunday newspapers, which include colour magazines.

There are also local newspapers, which only cover local news.

No national newspaper is owned or controlled by a political party.

Most newspapers have a definite political allegiance (left, right or centre) reflecting
   the views and interests of their owners.

There is no censorship of newspapers, but editors can be sued for libel or
   defamation (stories that damage someone's reputation).

There is no fixed price for newspapers.

Newspapers are available on the Internet.

55% of adults read a national newspaper every day.

Young people tend not to read newspapers.

3 Look at the front pages of these newspapers. They were all published on the same day.

a Which of these newspapers seems to be the most 'serious'?

b Which seems to be the most entertaining?

c One is a 'quality' paper, covering a wider range of news in greater depth. One is a 'middle market' paper, narrower and more superficial in its approach. The third is a 'popular' paper, even more superficial and sensational. Can you guess which is which?

d The daily sales figures for these newspapers are:

1.2m   4m   0.4m

Can you guess which figure goes with which paper?

4 Some British newspapers are hostile to further integration of Britain with Europe. They claim that Britain's freedom is threatened by European institutions. In order to turn British public opinion against Europe they publish stories about how the European bureaucrats ('Eurocrats') plan to destroy popular British traditions. Here are some examples. For each one, try to decide

– why this story might seem threatening to the people of Britain.

– whether the story is true or false.

a Fishermen must wear hairnets when they work.

b For reasons of hygiene the Royal Navy must abandon its tradition of stirring its Christmas puddings with wooden oars and use plastic oars instead.

c All Christmas trees must be a standard colour, symmetrical in shape, and with regularly spaced needles on the branches.

d Selling curved cucumbers will soon be illegal. All cucumbers must be straight, and genetic engineering projects are being encouraged to produce them.

e The European Commission has defined a maximum permitted noise-level for lawnmowers.

f Cricket clubs can no longer serve afternoon tea to their players during matches because of hygiene restrictions.

g Popular flavours of potato crisps such as 'prawn cocktail' and 'cheese and onion' will soon be banned by European legislation on food additives.

OPTION

Compare a British 'quality' newspaper to one from your country.

Consider these aspects: news (national and foreign), opinion, business and economics, cultural pages, other non-news pages (e.g. fashion, health, computers), design, advertisements, price.

D   BOOKS

I Look back to your questionnaire on page 60.
What type of book appears most often on your list?
Compare your results with others in the class.

One of Britain's best-known poets is Roger McGough. His work is enjoyed by people of all ages – both children and adults – in many countries. He began his career in the 1960s as a performer in the Liverpool pop group The Scaffold and he continues to tour and perform widely. The poems are meant to be read aloud – they are simply structured, easy to understand, full of comic rhymes and word-play – but their light-heartedness and ease often hide a serious point.

2 ⬭⬭ Here is a recent poem. Read it to yourself while you listen to the author reading it on the cassette.

What do you see in your mind when you read this poem?
What social problems does it deal with?
Do you think there are any useful suggestions in the poem for solving these problems?
Write down your thoughts, then discuss them with a partner.

Five-car Family

We're a five-car family
We got what it takes
Eight thousand cc
Four different makes

One each for the kids
I run two
One for the missus
When there's shopping to do

Cars are Japanese of course
Subaru and Mazda
And the Nissan that the missus takes
Nippin down to Asda

We're a load of noisy parkers
We never do it neat
Drive the neighbours crazy
When we take up half the street

Unleaded petrol?
That's gotta be a joke
Stepping on the gas we like
The smoke to make you choke

Carbon monoxide
Take a deep breath
Benzine dioxide
Automanic death

'Cos it's all about noise
And it's all about speed
And it's all about power
And it's all about greed

And it's all about fantasy
And it's all about dash
And it's all about machismo
And it's all about cash

And it's all about blood
And it's all about gore
And it's all about oil
And it's all about war

And it's all about money
And it's all about spend
And it's all about time
That it came to an end.

3 Listen to this interview with Roger McGough. As you listen, make notes about Roger McGough's life and work.

Compare notes with a partner. What do you find most interesting or surprising in what Roger McGough says?

4 Look at this list of recent best-selling books in Britain.

❶ THE GOD OF SMALL THINGS Arundhati Roy (Flamingo £6.99)
A novel about family life in India.

❷ LONDON: THE NOVEL Edward Rutherford (Arrow £7.99)
A novel of suspense, love and adventure over 2,000 years in London.

❸ BRIDGET JONES'S DIARY Helen Fielding (Picador £5.99)
A comic novel about a young woman trying to enjoy life while controlling her appetites.

❹ THE LITTLE BOOK OF CALM Paul Wilson (Penguin £1.99)
A book of simple 'recipes' for staying calm.

❺ LARRY'S PARTY Carol Shields (Fourth Estate £6.99)
An ironic novel about the life of a typical modern man.

❻ THE PROMS GUIDE 1998 (BBC £3.50)
A guide to London's biggest classical music festival.

❼ CAPTAIN CORELLI'S MANDOLIN Louis de Bernières (Minerva £5.99)
A novel set in Greece in World War II.

❽ WINDFALL Penny Vincenzi (Orion £5.99)
A novel about a woman who finds independence, then problems, when she inherits a fortune.

❾ BEFORE I SAY GOODBYE Ruth Picardie (Penguin £5.99)
Letters, articles and e-mails of a young journalist dying of cancer.

❿ COLD MOUNTAIN Charles Frazier (Sceptre £6.99)
A novel set in America at the time of the Civil War.

⓫ UNNATURAL EXPOSURE Patricia D Cornwell (Warner £5.99)
A thriller about murder by smallpox in Virginia and Ireland.

⓬ FERMAT'S LAST THEOREM Simon Singh (Fourth Estate £5.99)
The story of how a great mathematical riddle was solved.

⓭ ANGELA'S ASHES Frank McCourt (Flamingo £6.99)
An autobiographical account of growing up in Ireland.

⓮ CHLOE Freya North (Arrow £5.99)
A novel about a girl discovering 'love, lust, life' in a journey around Britain.

⓯ LONGITUDE Dava Sobel (Fourth Estate £5.99)
The history of how a great navigational problem was solved.

⓰ THE DIVING-BELL AND THE BUTTERFLY Jean Dominique Bauby (Fourth Estate £5.99)
The thoughts and memories of a man paralysed by a stroke.

⓱ GRACE NOTES Bernard MacLaverty (Vintage £6.99)
A novel about a woman whose music helps her survive family difficulties and depression.

⓲ HUMAN CROQUET Kate Atkinson (Black Swan £6.99)
A comic novel about a strange family.

⓳ MEN ARE FROM MARS, WOMEN ARE FROM VENUS John Gray (Thorsons £8.99)
A guide to improving communication between men and women in relationships.

⓴ WOMAN TO WOMAN Cathy Kelly (Headline £5.99)
A novel about two women struggling with love and marriage in Ireland.

5 What type of book (novel, history, thriller, guide or autobiography) appears most often in this list?
What are the best-selling topics or themes on this list? Are you surprised by any of them?
Do any seem 'typically British'?

6 Work with a partner and devise an idea for a best-selling novel or thriller for the British market.

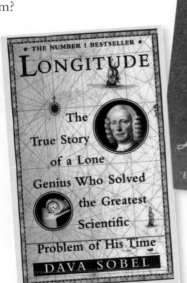

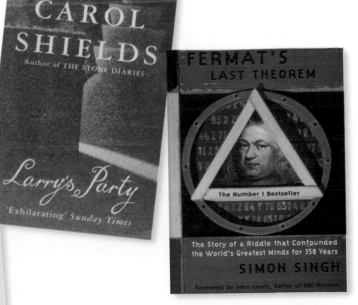

UNIT 8 HOLIDAYS

A SCHOOL HOLIDAYS

1 Work in pairs.

PARTNER A	PARTNER B
You are yourself.	You are a British person, of the same age as yourself.
Answer the questions for yourself.	Guess what a British person's answer would be.

Consider and discuss the questions in the box.

Do you holiday in your country	OR	in another country?
Do you prefer holidays abroad	OR	in your own country?
Do you prefer holidays with parents	OR	with friends or school?

Compare notes with the class. Were there many differences between your answers about yourselves and your guesses about a British person's answers?

2 Think of a few questions to ask a British teenager about holidays. Write some of your questions on the board.

3 ⬤⬤ Listen. Five British teenagers talk about their holidays. Which of your questions are answered on the cassette?

4 Here are some possible attitudes to holidays. Which ones are expressed by the teenagers? Listen again if you like.

a It's natural to stop going on holidays with your parents as you get older.
b Students like going on trips with their school.
c Going with friends is not so luxurious as going with parents.
d Going on holidays is expensive – we can't always afford it.
e Going with brothers or sisters who are close to our age is enjoyable.
f Most people don't like going abroad.
g Going with parents is not so much fun as going with friends.
h Holidays are a waste of time and money.
i The place you go is more important than the people you are with.

5 Can you sum up what the British teenagers think about going on holiday? Are their thoughts and experiences different from your own or similar?

6 Do most people in your class prefer active holidays, or lazy holidays? Find out how many in the class like

> tourist activities. e.g. visiting historic monuments
> sporting activities
> adventurous activities. e.g. climbing mountains, exploring caves
> lying on a beach
> sitting beside a pool
> holidays in hot places
> holidays in cool places
> a mixture of active and lazy days.

7 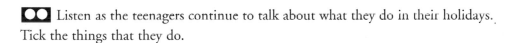 Listen to the British teenagers talking about the kind of holiday they prefer. How many of them prefer each kind of activity in the list above?

8 Are there times in your school holidays when you are not away from home?
Do you like to do any of the activities below? Or others?
Make a list of the three things you do most frequently in your school holidays.

| go to the cinema | go shopping | watch television | get a job |
| visit friends | read | do homework | help my parents |

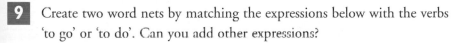 Listen as the teenagers continue to talk about what they do in their holidays. Tick the things that they do.

9 Create two word nets by matching the expressions below with the verbs 'to go' or 'to do'. Can you add other expressions?

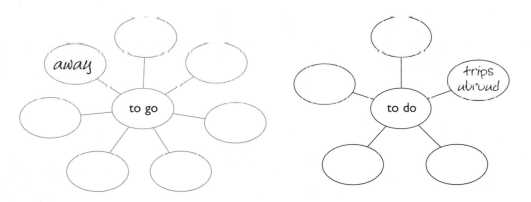

away
on trips abroad
on holiday
to Berlin
with your free time
with my parents
quite a bit of tourism
and stay with friends
something active
a bit of both
to see my grandmother
to dark places

Before you go on to the next part, think about holidays in the days of your grandparents.
Did they have holidays at all? What were the popular places for holidays? Did they take long holidays, or one-day breaks? Did they go to other countries? Try to find out as much as you can about holidays in the past. Look up history books or encyclopedias. Ask your parents or grandparents.

B   PAST AND PRESENT

Donkeys on the Beach.

1   What information did you find out about holidays in the past in your country? Did your grandparents go on holiday? Share what you know with the class.

2   Choose one of the pictures but don't say which one. Tell your partner

– one thing that someone is wearing.
– one thing that someone is looking at.
– one thing that someone is doing.

Can your partner guess which picture you are thinking of?

3 Look at the table on holidays now and in the past in Britain. Can you fill in any information from the photos?

	Holidays in the past	Holidays now
Destination		
Number of holidays		
Holiday clothes		
Holiday activities		

4 Look at the graphs and the table. Add more details to the table.

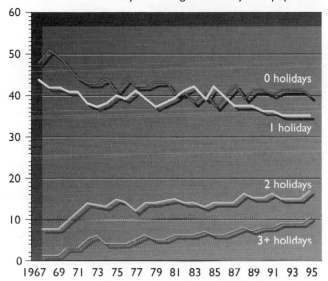

Number of holidays taken per year
Number of holidays of 4+ nights taken by % of population

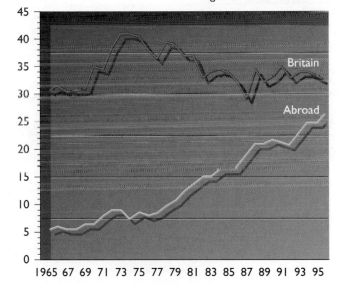

**Number of people taking
holidays in Britain or abroad**
No. of people (in millions) taking holidays
of 4+ nights in Britain or abroad

5 What is the most surprising thing for you

– about the photos?

– about the other information you have about holidays in the past?

6 Are holidays better now? List reasons for thinking that

– holidays are better now.

– holidays were better in the past.

Compare your ideas.

C   PICNICS

1 Do you enjoy picnics? Can you remember one from your childhood? Tell others about it.

Where did you go?	What did you wear?
How did you get there?	What did you eat and drink?
Who was with you?	Did anything go wrong?

2 Work with a partner.
Take these roles in turn.

ROLE 1	ROLE 2
You are a character in the picture.	**You are yourself.**
Answer your partner's questions.	**Ask your partner the questions above.**

3 Read the extract from the Irish writer Roddy Doyle's novel *Paddy Clarke, Ha, Ha, Ha* then retell
the story from the point of view of the mother or the father.
In small groups, choose one of these options. Prepare and present a short dramatic scene to the class.

a Paddy's picnic.
b An adaptation of Paddy's picnic set in your country.
c A picnic in the past.
d Your favourite picnic or your most disastrous picnic.

We went on a picnic the next day. It was raining but we went anyway; me and Sinbad in the back, my ma beside my da with Catherine on her knee. Deirdre wasn't born yet then. My ma's belly was all round, filling up with her. We went to Dollymount.

—Why not the mountains? I wanted to know.

—Stay quiet, Patrick, said my ma.

Da was getting ready to go from Barrytown Road onto the main road. We could have walked to Dollymount. We could see the island from where we were in the car. Da made it across and right. The Cortina jerked a bit and made a noise like when you pressed your lips together and blew. And something scraped when we went right in to the kerb.

—What's that sound from?

—Shhh, said Ma.

She wasn't enjoying herself; I could tell. She needed a decent day out.

—There's the mountains, I said.

I got between her seat and his seat and pointed out the mountains to them, across the bay, not that far.

—Look.

—Sit down!

Sinbad was on the floor.

—There's forests there.

—Stay quiet, Patrick.

—Sit down, you bloody eejit.

Dollymount was only a mile away. Maybe a bit more, but not much. You had to cross over to the island on a wooden bridge; the rest was boring.

—The toilet, said Sinbad.

—Jesus Christ!

—Pat, my ma said to my da.

—If we go to the mountains, I said, —he can go behind one of the trees.

—I'll swing you from one of the trees if you don't sit down out of my light!

—Your father's nervous –

—I'm not!

He was.

—I just want a bit of peace.

—The mountains are very peaceful.

Sinbad said that. The two of them laughed, Ma and Da in the front, especially Da.

We got there, Dollymount, but he had to drive past the bridge twice before he could slow down enough to turn onto it and not miss it and drive through the sea wall. It was still raining. He parked the car facing the sea. The tide was way out so we couldn't see it. Anyway, with the engine off the wipers weren't working. The best thing about it was the noise of the rain on the roof. Ma had an idea; we could go home and have the picnic there.

—No, said Da.

He held the wheel.

—We're here now, he said, —so –

He tapped the wheel.

Ma got the straw bag up from between her feet and dished out the picnic.

—Don't get crumbs and muck all over the place, Da said.

He was talking to me and Sinbad.

We had to eat the sandwiches; there was no place to hide them. They were nice; egg. They'd gone real flat; there were no holes left in the bread. We had a can of Fanta between us, me and Sinbad. Ma wouldn't let us open it. She had the opener. She hooked it under the rim of the can and pressed once for the triangular hole for drinking out of and again, for the hole on the other side for the air to go into. After a few slugs each I could feel little bits of food in the Fanta; I could feel them when I was swallowing. The Fanta was warm.

Ma and Da said nothing. They had a flask with tea in it. There was the cup off the top of the flask and a real cup that Ma had wrapped in toilet paper. She held out the cups for Da to hold so she could pour but he didn't take them off her. He was looking straight in front of him at the rain milling down the windscreen. She didn't say anything. She put one cup down and filled it, over Catherine's head. She held it out; Da took it. It was the big cup, the one off the flask. He sipped it, then he said Thanks, like he didn't mean it.

—Can we get out?

—No.

—Why not?

—No.

—It's too wet, said Ma. —You'd catch your death out in that.

D   HOLIDAYS AND TOURISM

1 What are the most visited places in your country? Make a list.

2 What are the benefits of having tourists visiting those places? What are possible disadvantages?
Make notes in small groups. Write some of your conclusions on the board.

3 What do people in your class feel about tourism? Are its advantages greater than its disadvantages?
Which of these statements would you agree with? Tick the appropriate column.

		Agree	Disagree
1	The need to protect nature and historic buildings is becoming more and more urgent.	◯	◯
2	Many beautiful places are already being destroyed by crowds of tourists.	◯	◯
3	Tourism is a major source of income for our country.	◯	◯
4	Some of the most famous places are so heavily protected that visitors can no longer enjoy them.	◯	◯
5	Let the tourist market develop without restrictions: everything will be all right in the end.	◯	◯
6	Governments should make sure that as many people as possible can visit tourist sites.	◯	◯
7	The only way to keep our heritage for future generations is to limit the number of tourists.	◯	◯

4 Here are the top ten tourist attractions in Britain, with the number of visits they get every year.

1	Blackpool Pleasure Beach	7,200,000
2	British Museum, London	5,896,692
3	Strathclyde Country Park, Motherwell	4,380,000
4	National Gallery, London	4,301,656
5	Palace Pier, Brighton	3,500,000
6	Alton Towers Pleasure Park, Staffordshire	3,011,000
7	Madame Tussaud's Wax Museum, London	2,631,538
8	St Paul's Cathedral, London	2,600,000
9	Funland and Laserbowl, Trocadero, London	2,500,000
10	Tower of London	2,407,115

Work with a partner. How many of the ten attractions can you match with their pictures?

5 Has anyone in your class been to any of these attractions?
Tell the others about it. Did you enjoy it? Was it very crowded?

6 Read the article about tourism in Britain.

The issue of how our heritage is to survive ever greater inundations of tourists becomes more and more pressing.

The inundation is happening here and now. London has run out of hotel rooms, Heathrow has run out of tarmac. Think of the impact made already, and multiply all that by 10: that gives some indication of the mighty tide of tourism we will face in the early years of the next century.

They will flock through Leicester Square and Piccadilly Circus, and the effect will be merely decorative. But they will also go to the National Gallery, the Victoria and Albert Museum, Stratford-on-Avon and Stonehenge. A minority – but a stunning number of people all the same – will go to the Lake District, too.

But this is not just a problem for the future. Under the press of numbers, many tourist experiences are already being destroyed. Everyone gets to see the picture, the monument, the palace but no one gets to see it properly. Everyone goes to Venice, but all you can think about while you are there are the jams of people seeing it with you.

The result is the progressive closing-off of sensitive sites. No one today can climb the tower of Pisa, walk among the columns of the Parthenon, or explore freely the colleges of Oxford. To our children, such experiences will be as mythic and improbable as driving on traffic-free roads or looking round unlocked country churches. The danger is that more and more of the planet's cherished places will suffer the same fate: disappearing under immense crowds, then being 'rescued' with the result that no one is able to enjoy them at all.

Allowing the tourist market to take its course unimpeded makes no more sense than allowing loggers to have their way in Amazonia. For any particular monument, the natural or man made, there is an optimum number of people who can enjoy it to the full at any given time. *Mona Lisa*, 5; Stonehenge, 50; Venice, perhaps 10,000. The task ahead for those who administrate such places is devising ways that will permit access to the right sorts of numbers, so that each person who pays their entrance fee will do so confident that they will be able to enjoy it to the full, in the same way that they enjoy the theatre or cinema, confident of having a seat with a view.

The challenge of the future will be to allow all who want it the most intimate possible contact with our heritage, while making sure that future generations will be able to enjoy it in the same way. Those twin goals will be impossible without a widespread and intelligently administered form of time ticketing.

The Guardian

7 Look again at the seven statements in Exercise 3. Put a cross in the columns to show which of them the author of the article agrees or disagrees with.
Are the opinions ticked for your class the same as those put forward in the article?
Would you favour a system of 'time ticketing' for the most popular tourist sites in your country?

8 If there was disagreement in your class, or between your class and the article, organise a mini-debate. In teams of four, prepare arguments for or against unlimited tourism in your country.

A   **THE PHYSICAL ENVIRONMENT**

1   Think about the geography of your country. Make notes about these features.

Mountains   Rivers   Seaports   Lakes   Forests

Lowland areas   Main farming areas   Areas of natural beauty

2   Look at the map on this page, and in Unit 1. Now write notes about Britain's geography.

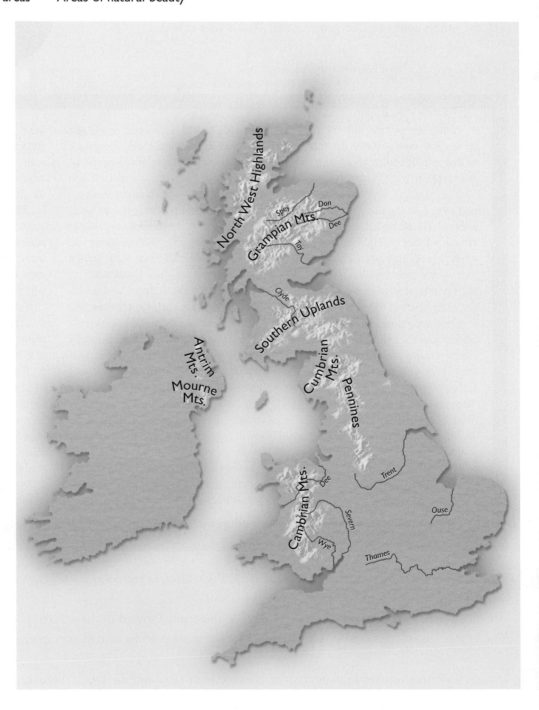

3   Make sure you know the meanings of these words. Look them up in the dictionary, if necessary, and see if you know the equivalent words or expressions in your own language.

cliff   estuary   resort
geology   granite   chalk
salt-marsh   sea-loch
(loch is the Scottish term
for lake)

Now read these two short descriptions of Britain's coasts, and look at the photographs. Can you identify each photograph from the text?

No one in Britain lives more than 120 km from the coast. Its cliffs and estuaries, its resorts and villages, and, less happily, its industries and their pollution, are part of the experience of most of its population. The coast, extending to 4,400 km in England and Wales alone [the total for Britain is over 7,000 km] possesses an infinite variety that owes much to the frequent changes in geology. Few other coasts can match the contrast between the granite cliffs of Penwith in Cornwall and the chalk cliffs of Flamborough, or the differing attractions of the dark sea-lochs of north-west Scotland, and the salt-marsh fringed estuaries of the Essex and Suffolk coasts.

John Chaffey,
A New View of Britain

One of the reasons for the great diversity of English beaches is the geological structure of the country. Inland, it needs a trained geologist to know what is going on. At the seaside, you only need a cliff cut away like a slice of layer cake to give you some idea of how – literally – the land is structured. So you have chalk ('young' rock, only up to 225 million years old) on the South Coast – which is those famous White Cliffs of Dover, for example, and the even more impressive Seven Sisters – and in Cornwall you have granite that can be as old as 600 million years.

Bryn Frank,
Everyman's England

4 Choose one of the places in the pictures.
Imagine you are visiting. What can you see?
What kind of place is it? How does it make you feel?
Write a postcard to a friend describing your visit.

B THE WEATHER

1 Here are some facts about the weather in Britain.
Which do you think are the most important for a visitor to know?

"Soon be autumn – the rain's getting colder"

a The climate is temperate, neither very hot in summer (average temperature 15 Centigrade) nor very cold in winter (average 5 Centigrade).

b The weather often changes rapidly throughout the day.

c There is no dry season.

d The weather is a favourite topic of conversation in Britain.

e The west of Britain has much more rain than the east: typically about 400 cm per year, compared to 60 cm.

f Britain lies in the zone of contact between tropical and polar air. This makes its weather very complex and difficult to predict.

g There are at least 150 weather forecasts every week on the five main British television channels.

h In winter there is often heavy snow on the hills and mountains, but little or none in the lowlands.

i In summer the sunniest and warmest places in Britain are on the south coast. They get around 1,700 hours of sunshine a year, compared with totals of 1100 to 1200 hours further north.

j In winter, the east of Britain tends to be colder than the west.

What practical advice would you give to a visitor about the weather in Britain?
What clothes should they bring – in summer? in winter?
What advice would you give a British visitor to your country?

2 Listen to this weather forecast, and write down what the weather will be like in these places.

Place	Today	Tonight	Tomorrow
East Anglia, Lincolnshire, North East England			
North West England, Midlands, Wales, Southern England			
Northern Ireland, Scotland			

Which of the facts about the weather (Exercise 1) are confirmed by this forecast?

3 Why do people in Britain talk about the weather so much? Read the four opinions on the opposite page, then match each one with one of the summaries.

a Jim (from Canada):

I think the British are more obsessed with the weather than many other nations because they live in a place where three major weather systems come together. That means that their weather is unpredictable, so they try to explain it to themselves by discussing it and exchanging theories, predictions and superstitions.

b Semira (from Morocco):

For me it's just a way of opening a conversation, in a friendly way. Foreigners sometimes don't understand. If you say 'It's a nice day', to a Moroccan he would be puzzled, because in Morocco nobody says it. Good weather is taken for granted.

c Tunji (from Nigeria):

I think there's a cultural reason. The British are a reserved people, they're not warm or outgoing, and there isn't a lot of personal contact between them. I can walk into my neighbour's house in Lagos and talk about anything I like. In London, people have to find something of common interest to talk about. Perhaps if they had problems to talk about they wouldn't bother to talk about the weather.

d Sarah (from England):

When you meet people for the first time, you know very little about them. You have to make some predictions – are you going to like them? Will they be interesting? One way of doing this is to talk about something neutral, something you both know about and really do have some interest in, but use the conversation for information about the other person. You choose a topic like the weather, and you then observe very carefully how the person talks about it.

1 The weather is complicated, so people need to share their opinions of it.
2 It's tradition: they are famous for discussing the weather.
3 It can seem strange to foreigners, but it's the British way of making people feel at ease.
4 It's a kind of code British people use to find out about each other.
5 It's a non-personal subject which provides a useful topic of conversation.

What about your country? Do people often talk about the weather? Do you know why?

4 A crossword. All the answers are in the weather forecast in Exercise 2.

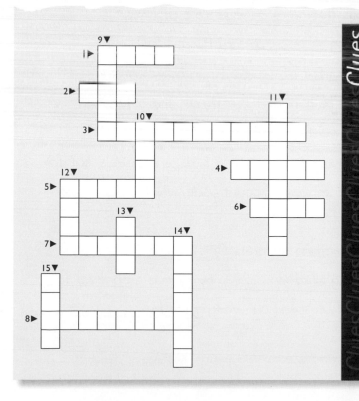

Clues

Across ▶
1 When it's _____ the weather is good. (4)
2 It's hard to see when this is around. (3)
3 The measure of heat and cold. (11)
4 No clouds in the sky. (5)
5 This hides the sun. (5)
6 Power for sailing boats. (4)
7 These are marked on thermometers. (7)
8 Bright days are full of this. (8)

Down ▼
9 This makes the ground white on winter nights. (5)
10 Not too harsh. (4)
11 When it's _____, you find ice on rivers and ponds. (8)
12 This is how you often feel in winter. (4)
13 When there's no rain, the ground becomes _____. (3)
14 Light bursts of rain. (Often seen in bathrooms!) (7)
15 Tiny particles of water in the air, often seen on autumn mornings. (4)

C   ATTITUDES TO NATURE

1   What does the word 'nature' mean to you?
How would you translate it into your language?
Write down its meanings and associations in
the word-tree on the right.

2   ▭▭ On the cassette you will hear three people
talking about nature. Write down the key words.
Are any of them similar to yours?

3   ▭▭ Listen again. Fill in the missing words
in the transcript.

Richard   Nature is basically those things in the world that man doesn't ...., that he

can with privilege .... from time to time, from afar or close, by being

................; but they are those things that carry on regardless of him.

Alex   Do you think of nature as something ...., or something violent and ....?

Richard   I think of it as .... and friendly, but of course it can be violent and ....

to man, such as the sea, which can be both of those things, and often is.

Alex   Wendy, what associations does the word nature have for you?

Wendy   Nature to me is .... and flowers and .... and birds, and animals, but for

me to a lesser degree ...., and an area of countryside, which .... has

not ruined.

Alex   So it's something very ...., something restorative?

Wendy   Oh very definitely so. And something which is .... by man as a contrast to

the .... world in which most of us spend our working life now.

4 🎧 Listen to the second extract. How does Richard get close to nature? What about Wendy?

5 🎧 In the third extract, Richard and Wendy are asked if their attitude to nature is unusual in Britain today. Can you summarise their answers?

6 Look at the pictures and texts below.
Discuss with a partner which ones

– appeal to you
– seem strange to you
– could, or could not, have come from your country (why?)
– seem typically British in some way (how?)

1

Nature is so uncomfortable. Grass is hard and lumpy and damp, and full of dreadful black insects ... If Nature had been comfortable, mankind would never have invented architecture.

Oscar Wilde, 'The Decay of Lying' (1891)

2

Since the year 1914, every single change in the English landscape has either uglified it or destroyed its meaning, or both. Of all the changes in the last two generations, only the great reservoirs of water for the industrial cities of the North and Midlands have added anything to the scene that one can contemplate without pain.

W. G. Hoskins, *The Making of the English Landscape* (1954)

John Constable,
Boatbuilding near Flatford Mill

3

Surely I must have been unlucky about the rain! I spent eighteen months on the Pennine Way, walking it in bits and pieces. Mostly it rained – pouring rain, driving rain, rain that came down like stair-rods. I came to pray not for fine days, which seemed too much to ask, but for gentle and not-too-wetting rain. My maps became sodden. So did I ... In any conditions, however, it will always be an invigorating exercise for the limbs, a complete change of environment, the perfect tonic for a jaded mind and a cure for urban depression. If you want to 'get away from it all', here, ideally, is the escape. You can't get further from the familiar than on the Pennine Way. You live for a time in a new world, and you forget the other.

A. Wainwright, *Pennine Way Companion* (1997)

4

... Nature never did betray
The heart that loved her; 'tis her privilege,
Through all the years of this our life, to lead
From joy to joy: for she can so inform
The mind that is within us, so impress
With quietness and beauty, and so feed
With lofty thoughts, that neither evil tongues,
Rash judgements, nor the sneers of selfish men,
Nor greetings where no kindness is, nor all
The dreary intercourse of daily life,
Shall e'er prevail against us, or disturb
Our cheerful faith, that all which we behold
Is full of blessings. Therefore let the moon
Shine on thee in thy solitary walk;
And let the misty mountain-winds be free
To blow against thee ...

William Wordsworth, *Tintern Abbey* (1798)

D ENVIRONMENTAL ISSUES TODAY

I In Britain there are over 70 organisations which aim to protect wildlife and the environment. Here are statements from three of them. All are from leaflets inviting people to become members. If you were going to join one, which would you choose?

NATIONAL TRUST

For more than a century the National Trust has been protecting our countryside, coastline and historic buildings and gardens for the lasting enjoyment of everyone.

As a charity dependent on public support, the Trust relies on membership subscriptions for a significant amount of the money it needs to look after the places in its care.

Today the Trust cares for

- some 240,000 hectares (590,000 acres) of beautiful countryside and 550 miles of unspoilt coastline
- over 300 historic houses and gardens and 60 villages
- 466 Sites of Special Scientific Interest and 28 national nature reserves
- 1,000 scheduled ancient monuments, 25 wind- and water-mills and 25 industrial monuments.

The Trust protects all these places for ever, for everyone to enjoy – now and in years to come. A membership fee is a small price to pay for the lasting protection of these wonderful places. Your support is vital to our future. So join us today and help the Trust to continue its work of protecting our heritage.

Annual membership £27; under 26, £13.

Benefits: free admission to all National Trust properties in Britain; guidebook, newsletter and magazine; gift catalogue; welcome information pack

Ramblers Association

Going for a walk gives you a unique sense of freedom. Whether you're on a demanding moorland track or just taking the dog for a stroll, you are enjoying a recreation chosen by a quarter of the population.

The possibility of wandering free over open ground is regarded as a natural right in many countries. But what most of us in Britain don't realise is that it has taken over 60 years of dedicated lobbying by one highly effective pressure group to achieve what we now enjoy: a national footpath network, the mosaic of national parks, and rights of access to thousands of acres of open land.

We take them all for granted but without the persistent efforts of THE RAMBLERS working at parliamentary and local levels, they would not exist at all.

If you enjoy walking we think you'll agree that the subscription is a small price to pay to enhance the freedom of us all.

Annual membership £17; students, £8.50.
Benefits: 400 local groups nationwide offer organised walks, conservation and watchdog activities; annual handbook with details of places to stay, long distance footpaths and walking holidays; quarterly magazine; local newsletters; discounts in outdoor equipment shops.

ROYAL SOCIETY FOR THE PROTECTION OF BIRDS

- Birds need places to feed, nest and rest – but due to human activities, many of these places are being lost. The Royal Society for the Protection of Birds is the charity that takes action for wild birds and the environment. We strive to prevent our birds and wildlife from losing out.

- Today the beautiful wild birds of our countryside face more threats than ever before – even some of the birds that visit your garden. The RSPB needs more members so we can protect more birds under threat.

- Everyone loves the song thrush. But over the last 25 years their numbers on farmland have dropped by 73%. Many other birds we often take for granted in our gardens and the countryside – like the skylark and the tree sparrow – are showing serious decline. But with your support it could all be very different.

Annual membership £23; under 18, £13. Benefits: free access to over 120 nature reserves; Birds magazine quarterly; welcome pack with information and window sticker; free bird table – 'makes watching birds at home more fun!'; local events; practical conservation activities.

2 What methods do the leaflets use to persuade you to join? Find examples of
- use of statistics.
- financial benefits and gifts.
- appeals to a sense of history or national pride.
- appeals to the reader's emotions.
- appeals to a sense of social responsibility.
- claims to give good value for money.
- any other methods you notice.

Did any of these methods of persuasion influence your choice in the previous exercise? Which ones?

3 What environmental organisations exist in your country? Analyse a similar leaflet from one of them. How does it compare with the ones above?

4 Project: Create a publicity leaflet for an organisation – real or invented – campaigning for environmental protection in your community.

A   LIFESTYLES

1 Complete the following questionnaire with a partner. Answer the questions for your
own country. Then discuss the questions for Britain, and guess what the answers could be.

Young people in our country and in Britain: what is their life like today?

Do most youngsters	*Yes? or No?* In our country,	*Yes? or No?* What about Britain?
1 live with two parents?	....	....
2 have a computer?	....	....
3 play truant? (not go to school when they should)	....	....
4 watch TV every day?	....	....
5 like school?	....	....
6 have pocket money?	....	....
7 use a library quite often?	....	....
8 have a job after the age of 11?	....	....
9 care about the environment?	....	....
10 have money in a savings account?	....	....

2 Work in two groups.

GROUP A	GROUP B
Read Text A on page 93.	**Read Text B on page 94.**

Read the texts quickly to find the answers for Britain. Don't worry if you don't understand some words.
Check as many answers as you can.

3 When you are ready, join a student from the other group. Do not show each other your texts, or your
questionnaires. Complete all the answers for Britain by asking each other and answering the questions.

4 When you have completed all the answers for Britain, compare the two texts. Look at Text A. Using the context to guide you for words you don't know, choose a definition from the box for each word.

1	decadent	6	absent
2	to terrorise	7	'green'
3	a senior	8	thrifty
4	virtuous	9	fortnight
5	to assume	10	anxiety

a away, not present	**f** frugal, careful with money
b two weeks	**g** worry
c cares about the environment	**h** to frighten or fill with fear
d to suppose, to take for granted	**i** behaving well
e behaving badly	**j** an older person

5 Now look at Texts A and B. Find expressions in either text which mean

a the amount of money people have to use as they like: ....

b someone who knows how to use computers: ....

c where money comes from: .... of ....

d help to see things in a fair way, without exaggeration: .... into ....

e equipment or appliances that people can buy: ....

f families without any children: ....

g an activity done for pleasure: ....

6 Look at your questionnaires and the texts. Discuss these questions.

Which facts about young people in Britain today are similar to facts about your own country?
Are there facts which are very different?
Which fact do you find most interesting?

7 Here are paragraphs from three articles about the attitude of young people to money in 1997. Write a headline for each article. Then choose the best or funniest headline in your class.

1 Pocket money today is a lucrative affair, with British children spending on average £8.40 a week on food, toys and clothes, according to the first official investigation into how they handle their cash. The biggest spending was on food, which included sweets, crisps, soft drinks, ice cream and school meals which the children bought. Second on the list were leisure goods.

2 The junior world is divided between those who subsist on parental pocket money and those who help earn their keep. 'If you go into the real world and get yourself a job, that's when you're going to prove you're independent'. As they grow up, many believe that getting a part-time job is a valuable step towards greater responsibility. 'I work to pay my mobile phone bills and my share of the phone bill at home. It's fair because I can't expect my mum to do everything for me now', teenager Julia Press said.

3 Music is the central focus of teenagers' lives and their spending, a survey reveals today. A TSB survey shows that music is the single most important thing in the lives of nearly a quarter of teenagers. Teenagers could also be the most important thing in the lives of record companies: some boys spend more than £50 a month on music.

8 What about spending habits in your class? Make a list of the top spending items. Do you think that

– spending habits of young people are fairly similar in most countries today?

– having money is important, so that young people can feel independent?

B ISSUES

1 What do you think are the main issues that young people in your country are interested in today?

As a class, brainstorm ideas: write all possible answers on the board, without assessing or selecting any particular one.

2 ⬭⬭ Students in England and Scotland were asked the question: What do you think are the main issues young people are interested in today in Britain? Listen to their replies, and tick any idea you listed on the board. Make a note of other ideas that you didn't list.

3 Decide on a debate question. Choose one of these issues or write one of your own.

- The government should legalise drugs.
- Our country should do more to protect the environment.
- The homeless are the responsibility of everyone in the community.
- Young people should enjoy life without responsibilities while they can.
- Political studies should be part of everyone's education.

TEAM A	TEAM B
Decide on reasons to support the question.	Decide on reasons to oppose it.

Each person in Team A gives one reason, then Team B opposes it. The team that can keep on going longest is the winner.

4 Interview another member of the class. Ask them: What are your hopes and fears for the future? Take notes, and report to another group or to the class.

5 ▭▭ Listen to Scottish and English students answering similar questions. What similarities or differences can you note between your answers and theirs?

What do you find most interesting in their answers?

6 Imagine the clock has suddenly gone forward by 30 years. How has life changed? Is it better or worse than today? Write a short description of what you might see around you. Talk to others in the class about what they have written.

OPTION

> Collect the most interesting ideas and shape them into a poem.

7 Talk to older people – parents, friends, or teachers.

What issues most concerned them when they were your age?
What issues most concern them now?

After listening to the cassette and talking to people, do you feel you have more in common with younger people in other countries, or with older people in your own?

C | PRIORITIES

1 What are your personal priorities for the future? Fill in the questionnaire for yourself, then find the averages for your class.

Questionnaire – Student priorities

Show your priorities by writing in a number from 0 to 3.

0 = no importance to me at all
3 = very important

'Over the next fifteen years, which of the following values in life are priorities for you?'

	0 to 3		0 to 3
My own personal development	☐	Developing creative/ artistic talents	☐
Developing a career	☐	Starting my own business/company	☐
Time with close friends/relatives	☐	Giving time to non-profit organisations	☐
Having a family	☐	Another priority	☐
Rewarding leisure/travel	☐		
Gaining international experience	☐		
Exercising and personal fitness	☐		

2 Write a short article about the priorities revealed in your class survey. Consider the following questions.

What would your class like from a job?

Would you prefer a high salary and long hours, or a rewarding home life and time to develop as a person?

Is a balanced life style more important than earning a competitive salary and a chance to become a manager?

If you would like to compare your choices with those of students in ten different countries world-wide, see p. 95.

3 What about people who are already in full-time work? How do their priorities compare with those of young people thinking of their future? Read the newspaper editorial about a recent survey in Britain.

ALL WORK, NO PLAY
We've got the balance wrong

It began life inside the American expression 'gettalife'. Since then the word has developed a life of its own – as used by the stressed workaholic who sighs, 'I have no life'. In this new context the word refers to those rare moments of genuine living, to those fleeting seconds of 'quality time'. It can be spent anywhere – just so long as it's away from the office or the factory.

The conflict between life and work is laid bare in a survey published this morning by *Management Today*

magazine. It makes for compelling and timely reading. The survey reveals that employees across Britain, male and female, are cracking under the stress of work overload.

More than half of respondents report spending between 41 and 50 hours a week at work, with a further 25% staying in the office for more than 51 hours. Close to half say they find it increasingly hard to reconcile their work with their personal commitments. Fascinatingly, a quarter say they would

accept less money in return for more time. There is a time famine out there, and British workers are among the hungriest. *Management Today* has called its report The Great Work/Life Debate, acknowledging the two are now in permanent conflict. It's a useful contribution, for that's exactly what's needed: a great debate about the way changes in technology and the labour market have transformed the way we all work – and try to live.

The Guardian

Look through the article and put the expressions under the appropriate heading.

Life

....

....

....

....

....

Work

....

....

....

....

....

| rare moments   stressed workaholic   genuine living   no life   fleeting seconds of quality time   away from the office or factory   cracking under the stress   work overload   staying in the office   personal commitments   time |

4 The survey mentioned in the editorial identified ten things that people in full-time work most desired, and ten things that they regretted and felt that they had to sacrifice.
Can you guess what the ten things are in each list? Write as many ideas as you can on the board.
Then look at the 'Wishes and Misses' on p. 95.

5 The following is an extract from the novel *Junk*, by Melvin Burgess, about young people who decide not to follow the same route as their parents. The narrator, Gemma, has run away from home and is now living with other young people in a 'squat' (a house taken over by people who don't pay rent). Although Gemma says she doesn't need money, in reality she and her friends live by stealing and other illegal activities.

I'm flying, but a lot of people end up dead inside. You can't tell to look at them but as soon as they open their mouths you know they've lost it. They got murdered by life.

I look back at where I came from and I think, What a mess most people make of their lives. My dad. Too scared to live, too scared to die. He works all day for that firm, managing this, managing that. Apart from the fact that it's other people who do the work – I mean the real work, the making things; he just burns himself out making himself look important, he doesn't actually do anything. And he hates it. And what for? He makes this money and spends it on a new TV when the old one still works, or a new car because the one he's got is old, or he spends it on a holiday to get away and relax from that ghastly job he's got to have because he needs the money ...

I don't need money. It's the people who want things gotta work.

Imagine the thoughts that Gemma's father has about his life, and about the way his daughter lives. Talk about it with others, then write a letter putting his point of view. The letter can be from the father, or from you, as if you were Gemma's friend.

D PARENTS

I Work in two groups.

> **GROUP A**
>
> **Read Text A from a novel.**
>
> **GROUP B**
>
> **Read Text B from a play.**

What do you think of the texts?
Make some notes about the following.

> What the characters are like.
> What their relationship is like.
> What the characters are trying to obtain.
> Which of the characters you sympathise with most.

When you are ready, join someone from the other group. Compare your texts and talk about your reactions to each one.

Scene from the production of *Three Birds* at the Royal Court Theatre, London

Text A Melvin Burgess, *Junk*

This extract shows relations between Gemma and her parents before she ran away from home. Gemma has just come in after spending a night away, against her parents' wishes.

> When I got home the next day, all hell broke loose.
> My dad was wagging up and down the room. 'There must be limits ... there must be rules!'
> Mum was sitting on the edge of the chair with no lips trying not to cry.
> 'We all have to follow the rules, Gemma. When I forbid something I expect you to obey me ...'
> I tried to smile at my mum but she looked the other way.
> Then he came out with this real beauty. Listen to this: 'Her reputation is a girl's greatest asset.'
> Stone Age!
> 'What about her GCEs?' I said. 'What about her ability to put her lipstick on properly?'
> My mum tried to bring the conversation into the real world.
> 'Darling, you're too young –' she began.
> 'She'll have to learn!'
> 'What are we going to do, Gemma? Your father's right, there have to be rules. Surely you can see that?'

Text B Timberlake Wertenbaker, *Three Birds Alighting on a Field*

Stephen's garden. GWEN, *eighteen, is weeding, vaguely.* STEPHEN *is mowing the lawn.*

GWEN   What I've thought is first I'd fly to New York and spend a few weeks, and then I'd go up to New England and watch their leaves, what's it called, the Fall, then I'd go to Canada and meet Robert and we'd take that train that goes across the mountains and – is this a weed, I'm pulling it out anyway – then we'd go to Alaska –

STEPHEN   How are you going to live?

GWEN   I thought you'd pay for some of it, and then I'd work, waitress or look after children in Canada, they have children there, don't they?
(A silence.)
Can you pay for some of it?
(A silence.)
I'm going to be a very limited person if I don't see the world.

STEPHEN   There are lots of things to see in England.

GWEN   Oh, Daddy, Devon, the Lake District, BORING – Sheep. Then Australia, I want to study the Aborigines, New Zealand, Antarctica ...

STEPHEN   There are lots of sheep in New Zealand.

GWEN   Yeah, but they're not the same, they'll look different, I'm sure, they'll be more – well, they won't be English sheep. And then I could find a world cruise and work as a chamber maid back to England. Or maybe I'll stay in Australia, will you miss me? Or maybe I could stop in Morocco and take a camel across the desert ...

2   ◖▢◗ On the cassette, five Scottish students talk about relations with parents.
Listen to the whole interview. What is your overall impression?
Are relationships

– generally good?
– good within limits?
– poor?
– so different that you can't generalise?

3   ◖▢◗ Listen again. Here are some points made by the students.

While their own relations with their parents are good, they know of other cases which are very different.
Relationships can be good so long as some limits are observed.
Relationships between the generations are the same now as they were in the past.
A good relationship is based on compromise: 'give and take' on both sides.
All relationships are individual: no generalisations are possible.

Which of their points do you find most informative or interesting?
Are there other points that you found striking?

4   How do the experiences of the students compare with the fictional characters in the two texts?

ADDITIONAL MATERIAL

UNIT 3C, EXERCISE 1

Sports participation (ages 11–19) in UK: the top ten, with the percentages of people who chose them as favourites

1	swimming (53.3%)	6	badminton (22.9%)
2	football (39.7%)	7	basketball (22.4%)
3	cycling (31.6%)	8	rounders (21.6%)
4	ten pin bowling (28%)	9	ice skating (17.8%)
5	tennis (24.4%)	10	billiards/snooker (17.4%)

UNIT 4B, EXERCISE 1

a True. Nomura Bank owns 3,998 British pubs (March 1998 figure).

b False. Supermarkets have more than doubled their share of food sales in the past ten years.

c False. £1.26 billion is spent on hamburgers, but this is less than half of what is spent on medicines.

d True. Other figures concerning the national passion for potato crisps are: 5 kg per person per year = 292.5 million kg or 292,500 tonnes total consumption per year = 0.8 million kg per day = 33, 375 kg per hour = 556 kg per minute = 9.27 kg (185 bags @ 50 g) per second.

e True.

f True.

g True. The company is 'Iceland'.

h True. 52% are fast-food/takeaway restaurants. (1996 figures)

i False. The true figure is less than once a month. The total annual sale of ready meals from supermarkets is 500 million (1997).

UNIT 6A, EXERCISE 6

c 28 hours

UNIT 6A, EXERCISE 2

What people do – % participation – at least once a week

Activity	% of all people	% of 16- to 24-year-olds
Watching TV	96	97
Reading newspapers	80	72
Listening to the radio	73	73
Reading books	60	55
Listening to CDs/tapes/records	58	81
Watching videos (recorded programmes)	47	50
Playing with children	47	43
Gardening	42	12
Playing with pets	41	41
Reading magazines	40	45
Cooking for pleasure	37	38
Visiting a pub in the evening	36	59
Watching other videos	30	57

Source: *The Economist Britain in Figures*

UNIT 6C, EXERCISE 4

1 The average number of British productions is just above 100.

2 British film productions are increasing.

3 Successful British productions and co-productions in recent years include *The Full Monty* and *Shakespeare in Love*.

4 Yes, both directly and indirectly through the National Lottery funding.

UNIT 10A, EXERCISE 2, TEXT A

BRITAIN'S TOMORROW
Today's children are more virtuous than most assume

The picture painted by the Central Statistical Office's *Social Focus on Children*, shows that the decadent youths who terrorise their seniors are a tiny minority of young people. The old, virtuous habits of reading, learning and sport are by no means dead.

The report should also put into perspective current anxieties about the number of children being brought up by one parent. Four-fifths of dependent children, the CSO finds, still live in a family with two parents. They are, what is more, under more careful parental control than is often assumed: and most of them – three-quarters of 11- to 13-years-olds – actually like school. Even more say that their parents make sure that they do their homework. Although truancy is a problem for a small minority of the young, a surprisingly high 89% were never absent from school.

Seventy percent of children use a library at least once a fortnight, with half using it once a week. Sport is still very popular; even in winter, more than four out of five children play at least once a week.

So what will this generation be like as adults? Much 'greener' than their parents: nearly nine in ten are interested in the environment. Possibly thriftier: around three-quarters already have money in a savings scheme. Certainly computer-literate: 99% of primary-school children have hands-on experience of computers.

UNIT 6C, EXERCISE 6

a He did a directing course with the BBC.

b *The Samurai* by Melville.

c Being in control of the whole 'vision' of the film, including script, actors, shots, camera angles, design. Also having a chance to put his vision of life on screen. Quoting Orson Welles he compares a film-director to a child with a wonderful toy. He also says it is exciting and challenging.

d Interference by executive producers and TV companies. Compromise.

e In America directors are better paid, but there is more interference by the studio, which is very powerful; money is everything. Britain is moving in the same direction, but film-makers still have more freedom.

f *Cuts* seems a little old-fashioned in tone but is generally true: changing fashions mean sudden changes of mind, and money (represented by audience viewing figures) is far more important than truth or quality. He is amused by *Bridget Jones's Diary*, and thinks it accurately portrays the 'nerves and speed' of live documentary television, although this is a separate area of TV which he does not know well.

UNIT 10A, EXERCISE 2, TEXT B

A TV IN THE BEDROOM AND CASH TO SPEND

Most of today's children have money in their pocket and televisions in their bedroom. They worry about the environment, prefer the toys their parents enjoyed, and stay away from church.

Children's spending power is rising annually. For the first time in the 20 years in which records have been kept, girls are getting slightly more than boys.

However, particularly for older children, pocket money is not the only source of income and a quarter of those over 11 have a job of some kind. One 15-year-old in ten has at least £1,000 a year to spend and more than eight in ten have at least £5 a week.

Two out of five of those over 10 have a building society account and a further third in the age group have a bank account.

Homes with children also tend to be packed with consumer durables. Nearly six in ten households with children have a computer, more than four times the level in childless homes. Nine in ten children also go home to a colour television, video, washing machine and freezer. Watching television is the favourite pastime, with the average child watching three hours a day.

Soaps, particularly Neighbours, are popular and children generally prefer watching them to the special programmes made for them.

UNIT 10 C, EXERCISE 2

Answers given by students in the ten countries

Priorities on a scale of 0 to 3, where 0 is of no importance and 3 is very important

'Over the next fifteen years, which of the following values in life are priorities for you?'

	Average
My own personal development	2.49
Developing a career	2.37
Time with close friends/relatives	2.13
Having a family	1.93
Rewarding leisure/travel	1.82
Gaining international experience	1.75
Exercising & personal fitness	1.67
Developing creative/artistic talents	1.00
Starting my own business/company	0.83
Giving time to non-profit organisations	0.73

UNIT 10 C, EXERCISE 4

Wishes and misses

The top ten desires identified by the survey were:

1 Being able to work fewer hours
2 A change in the company culture
3 Work flexible hours
4 Reduce commuting – or avoid it
5 Work from home
6 Change jobs or relocate
7 More staff
8 Earn more
9 Retire
10 Reduce stress

Top ten sacrifices identified by the survey:

1 Missing out on children growing up
2 Putting work before home and family
3 Moving home for employer
4 Missed leisure/hobby time
5 Away from home – short term
6 Divorce/strain on the relationship
7 Away from home – long term
8 Time spent on work-related education
9 Not having/postponing children
10 Unable to form relationships

THANKS AND ACKNOWLEDGEMENTS

The authors would like to thank the following for their contributions to What's It Like?:

– all the teachers who worked with us and tested the materials for this book in many seminars in different parts of the world. Their comments were a crucial help in developing and shaping our ideas.
– the many friends and colleagues who provided support and help: Maurna Crozier of the Cultural Traditions Group in Belfast, Robert Rivington, Susie Healey, and Christine Townsend.
– our special thanks to Miriam Newman of Partners in Sound for her resourcefulness and energy in making recordings in schools in different parts of Britain.
– for their contribution to the recordings: Dr. Stuart Nuttall, Headmaster of Bablake School, Coventry; Joanne Collie's students at the Centre for British and Comparative Cultural Studies, University of Warwick; Richard Bailey, Jacqueline Dean, Tim Fywell, Roger McGough, Wendy Reid, Vera Ryhajlo, Andy Smith, Paul and Zarina Thapar.

At Cambridge University Press, we wish to thank Peter Donovan who set the project in motion, our editor James Dingle, and Alan Finch, Jo Barker, Geraldine Mark, Ruth Bell-Pellegrini, and Sandie Huskinson-Rolfe.

The author and publishers would like to thank the following individuals and institutions for their help in commenting on the material and for the invaluable feedback which they provided:

Alena Lhotáková, The Bell School, Prague, Czech Republic; Detlef Erdmann, Goethe-Gymnasium, Hamburg, Germany; Christiane Fraedrich, Institut für Lehrerfortbildung, Hamburg, Germany; Ernst-Albrecht Gajdus, Gymnasium Alstertal, Hamburg, Germany; Bernd Guth, Winterhude Comprehensive, Hamburg, Germany; Gertrude Buss-Hoch, Peter-Petersen-Gymnasium, Mannheim, Germany; Karin Fritsch, Weingarten, Germany; Elzbieta Genge, English Teacher Training College, Elblag, Poland; Hanna Gozdawa-Gołębiowska, English Teacher Training College, Warsaw, Poland; Olga Vinogradova, Moscow State 57th School, Moscow, Russia; Tatiana Oksenkrug, Secondary School 20/1239, Moscow, Russia; Lyubov Nikolayeva, Irene Burenkova and Galina Mishina, School 23, Vladimir, Russia; Selami Ok, Dokuz Eylül Üniversitesi, Izmir, Turkey.

The author and publishers are grateful to the following copyright owners for permission to reproduce copyright material. Every endeavour has been made to contact copyright owners and apologies are expressed for any omissions. In such cases the publishers would welcome information from copyright owners.

The Times for the article on p. 6 by Mary Ann Sieghart and the letter on p. 28 from Lord Harris, © Times Newspapers Limited (1995 and 1931); The Guardian for the articles on pp. 12, 19, 36, 45 (3), 75, 88, 95, © The Guardian; The Observer for the article on p. 13; Grace Nichols, 'Wherever I hang' on p. 18 from Lazy Thoughts of a Woman, Virago Press. Published by permission of Little, Brown and Company (UK); Terri Colpi, The Italian Factor on pp. 19 and 20, Mainstream Publishing Co. Ltd; Dilip Hiro, Black British White British on p. 19 and Roald Dahl, Charlie and the Chocolate Factory on p. 52, David Higham Associates; The Independent for the article on p.19 by Terry Kirby and James Cusack and on p. 45 by Diana Hinds; The Times Educational Supplement for the article on p. 20; J.A. Cuddon, The Macmillan Dictionary of Sport and Games on p. 23, Pan (1980); The Spectator for the article on p. 28 by Malcolm Muggeridge; Ian Wright, Mr Wright on pp. 28 and 31, published by HarperCollins Publishers; The Collected Essays, Journalism and Letters of George Orwell, Volume IV, In front of Your Nose 1945–1950 on p. 28. Copyright © by Sonia Brownell Orwell and renewed 1996 by Mark Hamilton, reprinted by permission of Harcourt, Inc. in the USA and by permission of AM Heath in the rest of the world; Robert Graves, Goodbye To All That on p. 29, permission granted by AP Watt Ltd on behalf of The Robert Graves Copyright Trust; The Guinness Book of Sports Quotations on p. 29 © Colin M Jarman and Guinness Publishing Ltd, 1990; Nick Hornby, Fever Pitch on p. 31, Copyright © 1992 by Nick Hornby. Published by Victor

Gollanz in the UK. Used by permission of Viking Penguin, a division of Penguin Putnam Inc.; Guide Bleu Grande-Bretagne on p. 33 © Hachette Livre; Derek Cooper, The Bad Food Guide on p. 33, published by Routledge; Antony and Araminta Hippisley Coxe, The Book of Sausages on p. 33, published by Victor Gollanz Ltd; Office for National Statistics, Official Handbook to Britain on p. 35 © Crown Copyright 1998; Shout Magazine for the article on p. 37/8, © DC Thomson & Co Ltd; JC Drummond and Anne Wilbraham, The Englishman's Food on p. 39, Jonathan Cape/Pimlico; Peter Hobday, The Simple Guide to Customs and Etiquette on p. 40, Global Books Ltd; Meera Syal, Anita and Me on p. 41, HarperCollins Publishers. US rights Copyright © Meera Syal 1996. Reproduced by permission of the author c/o Rogers, Coleridge & White Ltd., 20 Powis Mews, London W11 1JN; The National Curriculum on p. 43. Crown copyright is reproduced with the permission of the Controller of Her Majesty's Stationery Office; The Daily Mirror for the article on p. 45; Jonathan Harvey, Babies on pp. 46–7, and Timberlake Wertenbaker, Three Birds alighting on a Field on p. 91, Methuen; The Economist Pocket Britain in Figures on pp. 50 and 71, Profile Books 1996; Helen Fielding, Bridget Jones' Diary on p. 54, Picador 1996; Malcolm Bradbury, Cuts on p. 54. Copyright © Malcolm Bradbury, permission granted by Curtis Brown on behalf of the author; Rob Humphreys, The Rough Guide to London 2nd edition on p. 57 and The Rough Guide to Britain on pp. 58–9; The Big Issue (edition 197) for the article on p. 62; Roger McGough, Five Car Family on p. 66. Reprinted by permission of The Peters Fraser and Dunlop Group Limited on behalf of: ROGER MCGOUGH; Roddy Doyle, Paddy Clarke Ha Ha Ha on p. 73, published by Random House in the UK. Copyright © 1993 by Roddy Doyle. Used by permission of Viking Penguin, a division of Penguin Putnam Inc. in the USA; John Chaffey, A New View of Britain on pp. 76 and 77, published by Hodder Headline plc; Bryn Frank, Everyman's England on p. 77, published by J.M. Dent; WG Hoskins, The Making of the English Landscape on p. 81. Reproduced by permission of Hodder and Stoughton Limited; National Trust membership brochure 1999 on p. 82; The Ramblers' Association membership brochure 1999 on p. 82; The RSPB membership brochure 1999 on p. 82; Melvin Burgess, Junk on pp. 89–90, published by Andersen Press.

The author and publishers are grateful to the following illustrators, photographers, and photographic sources:

Illustrators: Gecko DTP: pp. 4, 5, 7 ,13, 35, 48, 76, 80; Phil Healey: p. 34 (b); Sheila Salway: p. 80; Martin Sanders: p. 6; Sam Thompson: pp. 28, 29; Kath Walker: p. 40.

Photographic sources: Allsport/Alex Livesey: p. 26 m; Allsport/Wayne McCullough: p. 18 bl; Alton Towers: p. 75 (i); Derby Day (oil on canvas) by William Powell Frith (1819–1909), Bonhams, London, UK/Bridgeman Art Library: p. 24 br, Donkeys on the Beach (postcard), Private Collection/Bridgeman Art Library: p. 70 tr, The Duke of Wellington at Waterloo (oil on canvas) by Robert Alexander Hillingford (1825–1904), Private Collection/Christie's Images/Bridgeman Art Library: p. 11 (9), The Oxford and Cambridge Boat Race, 1871 (litho), by Simpson, Private Collection/Bridgeman Art Library, credit: Wingfield Sporting Gallery, London, UK: p. 26 b, Boat Building by John Constable (1776–1837), Victoria and Albert Museum, UK/Bridgeman Art Library: p. 81 b, The Beach by Alfred Victor Fournier (1872–1932), Waterhouse and Dodd, London, UK/Bridgeman Art Library: p. 70 tl, Elizabeth I, Armada Portrait, c.1588 (oil on panel) by George Gower (1540-96) (attr.to), Woburn Abbey, Bedfordshire, UK/Bridgeman Art Library: p. 11 (6); Stewart Mark/Camera Press London: p. 55 (g); The J Allan Cash Photolibrary: p. 12 ml, mr, r, 22 r, 74 (e), 75 (f), (h); Collections/Nigel French: p. 4 bl; Donald Cooper (c) Photostage: p. 90; Sylvia Cordaiy Photo Library/Christine Hipkiss: p. 42 tl; James Davis Worldwide: p. 7 br; Ecoscene/Frank Blackburn: p. 77 mr; Environmental Images/Graham Burns: p. 86 br; Greg Evans International: pp. 7 tl, 24 t, 25 t, 58 br; Mary Evans Picture Library: pp. 11 (1); Eye Ubiquitous/Adina Tovy Amsel: p. 69, Eye Ubiquitous/Jason Burke: p. 68 b, Eye Ubiquitous/G. Daniels: p. 44, Eye Ubiquitous/Paul Thompson: p. 12 b, Saccha Lehrfreund/Format: p. 84 r; "Reprinted by permission of Fourth Estate Limited from Larry's Party by Carol Shields. Front cover image: detail from Presentiment by David Inshaw, courtesy of The

Bridgeman Art Library. Front cover design: Tracey Winwood (c) Fourth Estate 1988, Fermat's Last Theorem by Simon Singh. Jacket illustration by Andy Bridge incorporating portrait of Fermat (c) Academie des Sciences, Toulouse. Cover design by Tracey Winwood (c) Fourth Estate 1997, Longitude by Dava Sobel. Cover design adapted from an idea by Evan Gaffney. Portrait of Harrison by Thomas King used by permission of the Science Museum/Science and Society Picture Library, London. Photographs of clocks H-1 to H-4 reproduced by permission of the National Maritime Museum, London. Photograph of clock H-5 reproduced by permission of the Worshipful Company of Clockmakers Collection/The Bridgeman Art Library. Cover map by Pieter Goos (c) The Huntington Library, Art Collections and Botanical Gardens, San Marino, California Superstock": p. 67; Leslie Garland Picture Library: p. 7 mr, 59 t, Leslie Garland Picture Library/A. Lambert: p. 42 r; Sally & Richard Greenhill Photo Library: p. 14 b; Richard Greenhill: p. 4 br, Sally Greenhill: pp. 22 l, 43, 53; Channel Four/Ronald Grant: p. 31 b, Columbia/Ronald Grant: p. 55 (f), Eon Productions/Ronald Grant: p. 55 (b), Polygram Filmed Entertainment/Ronald Grant: p. 55 (m), United Artists/Ronald Grant: p. 55 (a); Michael Holford: p. 11 (3); Hulton Getty Picture Collection: pp. 70 br, 72; Jeremy Nicholl/Impact: pp. 36, 84 m, Simon Shepheard/Impact: p. 74 (b); The Kobal Collection: p. 55 (l); Columbia (courtesy Kobal): p. 55 (e),(h), Paramount (courtesy Kobal): p. 55 (d), Twentieth Century Fox (courtesy Kobal): p. 55 (c); Life-File/Nigel Shuttleworth: p. 50; Mirror Syndication International: p. 55 (n); Peter Jordan/Network: p. 18 tr, Justin Leighton/Network: p. 86 tr, Gideon Mendel/Network: p. 86 tl, Martin Meyer/Network: p. 48, Mark Power/Network: p. 41; David Noble Photography: p. 7 ml; Northern Ireland Tourist Board: p. 4 tl; 'PA' News/ Sean Dempsey: p. 24 bl, 'PA' News/Peter Jordan: p. 18 tl, 'PA' News/John Stillwell: p. 18 br, Steve Eason/Photofusion: p. 86 bl, Nicky Johnston/Photofusion: p. 89; Pictor International: pp. 7 tr, 14 t, 22 mr, 86 ml; Popperfoto: pp. 16 l, 26 t, 55 (i); Private Eye: p. 51; reproduced with permission of Punch Limited: pp. 34 t, 38, 78; Rex Features Limited: pp. 11 (11), 21 b, 55 (j), 66, Rex/Tony Kyriacou: p. 21 t, Rex/Dave Lewis: p. 55 (k); Jules Selmes: pp 17, 32; Skyscan Balloon Photography/Phillip Dolphin: p. 81 t; Spectrum Colour Library: pp. 4 tr, 57 t, 58 tr, 74 (a); The Still Moving Picture Company: p. 74 (d); Tony Stone Images/Oliver Benn: p. 74 (c), TSI/Augusta Butera: p. 68 t, TSI/David H. Endersbee: p. 57 r, TSI/Elizabeth Furth: p. 25 m, TSI/Susanne & Nick Geary: pp. 7 bl, 75 (g), TSI/Janet Gill: p. 4 ml, TSI/Paul Harris: p. 77 b, TSI/Mark Lewis: p. 84 l, TSI/David Madison: p. 22 ml, TSI/Michael Rosenfeld: p. 49, TSI/Kevin Schafer: p. 77 bm, TSI/Bob Thomas: p. 25 b, TSI/Charlie Waite: p. 77 t, Michael Powell/Times Newspapers Limited: p. 59 b; Topham Picturepoint: pp. 11 (10), 63, 70 bl, 75 (j), Associated Press/Topham: p. 16 r, 'PA' News/Topham: p. 31 t; John Walmsley Photo Library: pp. 42 m, 58 tl.

Our special thanks to Computer Active, Match of the Day, Q Magazine, Shout Magazine, The Spectator/Cartoon by Jonathan Wortridge, for permission to reproduce front covers for p. 60. The Express, The Guardian, The Sun Newspapers, for permission to reproduce front covers (25 May 1999), for p. 64.

t = top   m = middle   b = bottom   r = right   l = left

Cover photographs: Indians in deckchairs: Barry Lewis/Network; Trafalgar Square: TSI/Joe Cornish; Henley: TSI/Dan Smith; Morris Dancers: Eye Ubiquitous/David Cumming; Carnival: Eye Ubiquitous/David Cumming; Mountain climbers: Eye Ubiquitous/Bob Battersby; Kids eating fish & chips: Ulrike Preuss/Format.

Picture Research by Sandie Huskinson-Rolfe of PHOTOSEEKERS.

Design, production and reproduction handled by Gecko Limited, Bicester, Oxon.

Sound recordings by Miriam Newman of Partners in Sound.

Freelance editorial work by Alan Finch, Geraldine Mark, Jayshree Ramsurun.

Permissions clearance by Ruth Bell-Pellegrini.